THERE'S
MORE
TO LIFE
THAN
MAKING
A LIVING

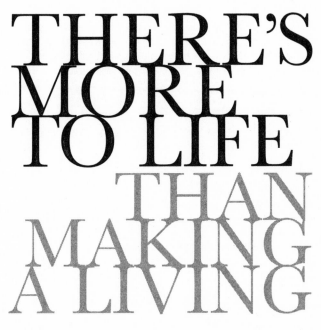

THERE'S MORE TO LIFE THAN MAKING A LIVING

Mastering Six Key Essentials on the Way to a Life of Significance

Jack C. McDowell

WITH PHIL NEEDHAM

Faith
Words

New York Boston Nashville

FaithWords
Hachette Book Group
237 Park Avenue
New York, NY 10017

Visit our website at www.faithwords.com.

Printed in the United States of America

First Edition: November 2009
10 9 8 7 6 5 4 3 2 1

FaithWords is a division of Hachette Book Group, Inc.
The FaithWords name and logo are trademarks of Hachette Book Group,
Inc.

Library of Congress Cataloging-in-Publication Data
McDowell, Jack C., 1930–
   There's more to life than making a living : mastering six key essentials
on the way to a life of significance / Jack C. McDowell ; with Phil
Needham. — 1st ed.
      p. cm.
   ISBN 978-0-446-55594-4
   1. Vocation. 2. Vocational guidance. 3. Work—Religious aspects—
Christianity. 4. Job satisfaction. 5. Conduct of life.
I. Needham, Phil, 1940– II. Title.
   BV4740.M294 2009
   248.4—dc22
                        2009007025

This book is dedicated to the officers and lay leaders of the Salvation Army who follow in the footsteps of its founders, William and Catherine Booth, and give their lives for its mission of compassion.

CONTENTS

FOREWORD

Jack C. McDowell is one of the most focused people I know. At the same time, he is one of the most caring. When he sets his mind to something, he is an irresistible force for good.

How did he become a phenomenally successful fund-raiser for charitable causes, a guru of community relations, and a counselor to countless young leaders of nonprofit companies? How did this farm boy from Minnesota with a disarming intensity find himself mobilizing community leaders to tackle fund-raising goals that few thought attainable—and to succeed, not only in reaching the goal, but also in exceeding it? Why is it that at seventy-eight years of age, he is still as relentless as ever in pursuing ways to make this world a better place and to help organizations like the Salvation Army serve the marginalized even more effectively?

This book is the fruit of Jack's amazing journey. It reveals his faith in God, his persistent pursuit of his calling, the significant people in his life and how they mentored him, the difficulties he faced and how he overcame them. In *There's*

More to Life than Making a Living, he shares the lessons he has learned and the keys to effectiveness and success he has acquired. Mastering these essentials will help you find life with purpose and personal fulfillment. They will show you how to use your unique abilities and opportunities to make a better world. They will teach you ways you can contribute to the lives of others through compassionate action. They will help you discover and live your own calling in life.

The reader who is interested in learning how others overcame weighty obstacles to find significance and fulfillment will find this book well worth the time. The reader who is looking for inspiration will find plenty to uplift. The reader who is looking for help to gain clarity about the mission to which God is calling him will find this book to be a valuable resource. The person who is looking for practical help in realizing his life's calling will find specific action steps he can take to do so. The reader who wants his or her life to count for others will find excellent clues. This book is both an inspiring story and a useful guidebook.

In these pages you will read about a thirteen-year-old boy who sought the face of God and prayed a prayer that piloted him for the rest of his life: "Help me, dear Father in heaven, to find a significant purpose for my life." The only child of a family that moved from California to a dilapidated farm in the north woods of Minnesota, he had responsibility thrown on him that very few teenagers see. During those hard years he wondered what life had in store for him. He seemed stuck in a world of limited horizons. His first taste of success on the "outside" came during his teenage years when he almost single-handedly raised the money for a new 4-H Club facility in the small town nearby. God had wasted no time in placing before this young man an opportunity to begin to discover his life's purpose.

He eventually moved to Texas where he conducted a number of successful fund-raising campaigns. A few years later he met a man named Harry Ward, a Salvation Army officer who needed to raise money for his organization's work in the Louisiana–Arkansas area where he was divisional commander. The young fund-raiser said he would help—and the rest, as they say, is history. Over the ensuing decades he raised millions upon millions of dollars for Salvation Army units across the Southeast. Not one of his campaigns failed to reach—and exceed—its goal.

God's calling found Jack McDowell, and Jack McDowell found a worthy purpose for his life. He was to use his genius for fund-raising and community relations and the self-discipline instilled during those early farm years to serve the millions of people touched by the ministry of the Salvation Army. Yes, he has been a brilliant fund-raiser, but that was not to be the sum total of his contribution. Wherever he went, he dedicated himself to raising the public profile of the Salvation Army, he strengthened its advisory boards, he mentored the younger leaders with whom he worked, and he was a voice for those without a voice.

Somewhere along the way, fortune smiled on Jack in another, most wonderful way. A beautiful lady from Salzburg, Austria, came into his life. Her name was Peggy, and she brought with her the world of opera and European art, as well as her own success in merchandising. Two very different worlds came together in their marriage: the American Midwest, a culture of new beginnings and hard work, and Salzburg, a culture of gracefulness and rich history. It was a marriage of opposites, blended by love. It still goes strong almost fifty years later.

During his early years on the farm, Jack would wonder what possibilities lay beyond the long dirt road of his farm world. One day, as a young adult, he traveled down that road for the last time. This time he kept going and didn't stop. He didn't return till twenty-five years later. It was a real homecoming, but without a crowd. He just wanted to be alone to remember his strong, loving parents and the incredible good those very tough years had done for him. He wanted to recapture that world for a brief time, then let it return to its honored place in the journey of his past. And finally, he wanted to look down that long dirt road again, and thank God for the way it had started him well on the way to a remarkable life.

—*Phil Needham*

PREFACE
The Long Dirt Road to My Calling

During my preteen to young adult years, my parents and I lived on a farm in northern Minnesota. That farm was my world. It kept me busy from sunrise to sunset. With an ailing father and no siblings, I carried the lion's share of responsibility for the outdoor farmwork.

Public school was a luxury in which I could only sporadically indulge. My home school was the pasture and the plow. My teachers were my parents and the discipline of the farm. I learned well. By the time I reached adulthood, I knew how to run a farm. My future seemed set. It would be played out in the small world of the Triple J Stock Farm. Or so it seemed.

A long dirt road ran from the farmhouse to the entrance gate. From there another long dirt road led to a very small town. I would often travel these dirt roads, wondering where they could eventually take me if I set out and didn't come back. Was there something out there beyond what I could imagine? The dirt road came to represent for me the entryway to my destiny, which I increasingly dared to believe lay beyond the boundaries of our farm.

It was while traveling that dirt road that I began to dream about the future and to ask God to help me find a significant purpose for my life. For thirteen years our farm's fences defined the perimeter of my world, a world in which I plowed the fields, planted the crops, milked the cows, and cut the wood. It was a world of simple things, hard work, and long hours. That long dirt road defined the journeys of my early life. My main contact with the outside world was when I walked the road to the mailbox. When I was able to go to school, I walked into town on that road. A big event in the spring and fall was the arrival of the Sears & Roebuck Catalogue, bringing with it the newest revelations from the outside world. It was the primary means by which we not only did our shopping but also saw changes that were taking place. During those years my world was remote. When the freight train passed the farm twice each day, I wondered where it was going and what excitement lay along its routes. As the steam engines were replaced over time by diesel, I sensed the larger world was also changing, passing our little farm community by.

As tough and isolated as those years were, I am grateful for them. They laid a solid foundation for my life. They taught me valuable lessons. They shaped my character and established my values. When I left the farm at the age of twenty-five, I was ready to find my destiny. I was ready for what lay beyond the long dirt roads of my youth.

In this book I want to share with you how I found a life of significance. Many choices lay before me. I could have gone other routes, and I am grateful to God that He opened the doors He did. He allowed me, not only to find a purpose for my life, but also to find significance.

I believe many people find a purpose for their lives without finding significance. They master certain skills, apply them effectively, and perhaps reap a harvest of success. But in moments of quiet honesty, they have a nagging feeling of emptiness. Something is missing.

A life of significance means that your life has positive meaning and value beyond individual success. It means that you have contributed to the lives of others and shared your compassion. It means that you have found the purpose for which we were all created: "'Love the Lord your God with all your heart and with all your soul and with all your mind' [and] 'Love your neighbor as yourself'" (Matthew 22:37–39).

Whatever your personality, whatever your life experiences, this is what will give your life significance. Whatever your gifts and abilities, this is your God-ordained purpose. Whatever your life has been like to this point, this is its purpose from here on.

In this book I will share with you Six Key Essentials for a Life of Significance. The section for each essential contains specific actions that will help you master that essential. These steps are the harvest of my own experiences, good and bad. They were gleaned from my many teachers and mentors. Most of all, they have been the gifts of a providential God to this seeker after a life with deeper and more lasting meaning.

You will notice that the first three essentials have primarily to do with important foundations to be laid, basic decisions to be made, lessons to be learned, and character qualities to be nurtured. The last three essentials have primarily to do with developing deep relationships, forging positive partnerships for good, and making your life count through your last day on earth.

I hope you find what I have learned on my journey to be

an encouragement and resource for your own journey. Please consider the following pages to be a personal invitation to you to discover that there is far more to life than making a living.

—*Jack C. McDowell*

THERE'S
MORE
TO LIFE
THAN
MAKING
A LIVING

FIRST KEY ESSENTIAL:

Find Your Calling

This first key essential helps you set the direction and define the character of your life. The company you work for, the position you hold, or the particular job you have may change. But your true calling does not depend on these matters, nor on your being the most successful in your field. Your calling is how you best use all God has given you—talents, passions, resources, opportunities, and experiences—to serve His gracious purposes in the world.

You are one of a kind. No one else is exactly like you. Finding your calling means discovering the unique contribution you are able to make to the betterment of others. It is figuring out how your competencies can be used to channel your compassion in the best ways. It is investing in a life of significance more than climbing the ladder of "success." It is moving beyond making a living to getting a life—a life you can look back on with gratitude and forward to with expectation.

The following five actions will help you find and define your calling.

ACTION:

Seek the Heart and Mind of a Providential God

I believe in the providence of God. This does not mean that bad things do not happen to good or innocent people. They do. What I believe is that every life has significance in the eyes of God and that whatever comes our way, good or bad, God is able to see us through to a fulfillment beyond current circumstances.

None of us need be outside His providential care. The apostle Paul wrote about a host of calamities that had befallen him and others like him, then concluded with the truth that overrules the power of those adversities: nothing, absolutely nothing, "will be able to separate us from the love of God that is in Christ Jesus our Lord" (Romans 8:39).

I have discovered how essential it is to believe in a God who loves me and wishes good for me. Such a God is someone I can trust. He is the One whose heart and mind I want to seek. He is the One who holds the key to the meaning and purpose of my life. As a lad on a farm in northern Minnesota, I began to believe in such a God.

Sometimes it was not easy.

SERIOUS SETBACKS

A few years after we moved to the farm, my father became very ill and several costly operations were required. We were forced to mortgage the farm to cover the cost of his hospitalization and medical expenses. His recovery was slow and his health was weakened. The situation required that I work harder than before. In addition to farming I began cutting wood to sell to increase our limited income. I did everything I could to earn money to pay the interest on the mortgage and meet our rising expenses.

One spring at calving time I began to notice something strange. Some of the calves were born deformed and others were born blind. Our dairy herd had contracted Bang's disease through artificial insemination. This dreaded disease had been carried on the boots of the artificial inseminator. Our herd was quarantined. We were put out of the dairy business. Our entire herd of registered dairy cattle was shipped to the packinghouse in Saint Paul, Minnesota.

On July 9, 1955, we had an auction and sold all the machinery and farm equipment. When the auction was over and the bills were paid, we had a total of $4,400 in cash and a $9,500 mortgage on the farm.

HUGE RESPONSIBILITIES

From the time I was fourteen, I prayed this simple prayer each day: "Dear Father, help me to find a significant purpose for my life." In spite of the seemingly insurmountable problems I had to cope with, I believed that I was not outside God's providence and that God would help me find the future that would give my life meaning.

As a young man of twenty-five, I was responsible for my

parents' welfare and their security. I was responsible for paying the farm mortgage and the mortgage on the machinery. I was responsible for making a living and supporting my parents for the rest of their lives. They had $4,400 in cash to live on until I could establish an earning capacity.

I had no education or training other than farming. I had followed my dad's admonition to do the best I could with what I had. I was afraid and didn't know what to do or where to go. I realized I had to leave the farm and find some way to make a living.

I began to review my experiences and the lessons I had learned from those experiences. I thought about the lessons Dad had taught me and the faith Mom had given me. They were unable to give me material gifts as we had so little money, but they gave me something far more precious: love and hope and encouragement. They had been my teachers and role models. They had taught me the most important lessons.

I was poor, but I had self-confidence because they believed in me and affirmed me. I was determined to honor their love by finding and achieving a worthwhile purpose for my life. I would always do the very best I could with what I had. I would seek to be worthy of their faith in me.

THE WAY FORWARD

As fate closed one door, providence opened another. I spoke with the local banker and told him of my problem and the responsibilities I had to assume. I explained that I now had to leave the farm and find a way to make a living to support my parents and myself. I said I needed some form of transportation and some money to live on until I could find work.

The banker owned the Ford dealership in Backus as well as

the Backus State Bank. He lent me the entire price of a new car and gave me three hundred dollars for living expenses until I could find work. He said I could pay him back as I was able and handed me the title to a new car. As we shook hands he said, "Jack, I know you'll succeed because I know what you've done with what you had. Don't be afraid, just do your best."

My fears increased as I said good-bye to Mom and Dad and left the farm where I had grown from a boy to a man. As I drove away I thought about the hardships we had endured, only to have all we had worked for lost. I was beginning a new life with the weight of responsibility and debt on my shoulders, and I was afraid. I drove to Dallas, Texas, because I had heard it was a city of opportunity. After renting a room in a boardinghouse for eight dollars a week, I began to look for a job.

My years on the farm and my work in 4-H had taught me valuable lessons, and I thought about how those lessons could help me at this time. I remembered my success in various speaking contests. I drew confidence from the memory of how as a teenager I had single-handedly raised the money to pay off the mortgage on the 4-H building. These kinds of experiences had taught me lessons that could help me build a future.

OPPORTUNITY GRASPED

One day I saw an advertisement in the newspaper that a company was looking for an additional fund-raiser. I answered the advertisement and received an appointment for an interview. When I met with the company's president, I explained what I had done in 4-H and the success I had had in helping the club raise money. I was offered the opportunity to become an assistant to a member of their firm.

This position gave me the opportunity to educate myself in a profession. I worked hard to learn as much as possible about fund-raising techniques. I asked every question I could think of and did everything I could to help the senior members of the firm. I studied what they did and evaluated the results they achieved. I noticed that in many instances they did the same thing even though the causes they were raising money for were quite different. They would spend a great deal of time telling others what to do, sitting in their offices and making plans for others to follow. Often the results fell far short of the goals that had been established and on which their fees had been based. I discovered that fund-raising fees, much like legal fees, were very high, often as much as 50 percent of the funds that were raised.

After a year I was given an opportunity to conduct my own fund-raising effort. It was a community United Way Campaign that the company had conducted for a number of years. In spite of the fact that the goals had never been reached, the company I was working for continued to be hired for the job. I was determined to exceed the goal if at all possible, and fortunately I did, by 5 percent. That year the company was credited with conducting one of the most successful campaigns in the state of Texas.

The opportunity that was to change my life came as the result of another failed campaign that had been conducted by the company I was working for. The contract period had expired and less than half the money had been raised. In fact, the cost of the campaign had exceeded the amount raised. My company asked me if I could do anything to salvage the effort.

I went to the community, met with the board of directors, and told them I would do my best if they would follow my directions. They agreed to do so. Six weeks later we reached 125 percent of the announced goal. This experience encouraged me to establish my own fund-raising company. The lessons I learned in raising the money for the 4-H building were becoming the foundation on which I would build my management-counseling and fund-raising business.

I named my company Community Development Service, and my first campaign was conducted for the Arkansas Enterprises for the Blind. The sponsoring organization was the Lions Clubs of Arkansas. My job was to coordinate the efforts of the members and encourage them to contribute the funds needed to construct three buildings for the Enterprises for the Blind in Little Rock, Arkansas. I visited every Lions Club in Arkansas. It was a wonderful experience! When the campaign was completed, we had raised 150 percent of the announced goal. Other church and college campaigns followed in the wake of this success.

While I was conducting the Enterprise for the Blind campaign, I received a call from the Salvation Army's divisional commander in New Orleans, asking if I would conduct a campaign for the Salvation Army in Hot Springs, Arkansas. I told him I would after I had finished the campaign in Little Rock and fulfilled several other commitments. It would be another two years before I could devote any time to the Salvation Army.

Two years later I did conduct that first campaign for the Salvation Army in Hot Springs. It was the beginning of a lifelong relationship with one of the greatest faith-based organizations in the world.

I had come through the overbearing discouragement of one failure after another on the farm to the beginning of personal success, yes, but more important, to partnerships that benefited a wide range of people. God had begun to lead me toward significance. I sensed His pleasure.

To the Reader:

I invite you to take seriously God's providential care for you, to seek His heart and mind as far as you are concerned, and to ask Him daily to help you find your way to significance. It may be helpful to ask yourself this question: *What is it that, when I do it, I feel God's pleasure, and He smiles?* Your answer may help you in your quest to find significance.

Note: It may be that up to this point in your life you have not given much time or thought to your relationship with God. You may not even be sure that you believe in a God who loves and gives notice to every person He has created. If this describes you, taking the step I've just described will probably be more difficult for you than for others. I can only say that without this step, my own discovery of a significant purpose for my life would not have been possible. I think it will be so for you, as well.

ACTION:

Allow Yourself an Extraordinary Vision

If you are going to find more to life than making a living, you must allow yourself an extraordinary vision. It does not need to be spectacular. In fact, if you are trying to be spectacular, you are probably missing the mark. The performance of a gifted athlete may be spectacular, but if he is not contributing to the success of his team, if he has not become a positive role model for aspiring young athletes, or if he is not using his success as an athlete as capital to benefit others, he is not living a life of significance. If, on the other hand, he uses his position and talents to exert a positive influence for good in the world, he may not be spectacular, but he is definitely significant. He has found an extraordinary vision, and he is guided by it.

Performing in an *extraordinary* manner simply means not confining oneself to doing the expected. It is ordinary to follow the job description, to put in the minimum time and effort, to do only what is necessary to make a living. It is ordinary to stick to an agenda of self-advancement. It is ordinary to color inside the box.

It is extraordinary to have a vision beyond oneself, to live for a larger purpose than personal success, to fully embrace opportunities to share compassion. An extraordinary vision is a God-given vision for your life.

The temptation is to be timid about the possible significance of your life—for a homemaker to think that she is only a homemaker rather than a molder of character, a nurturer in a world who takes without giving, a teacher who models caring beyond the borders of family. A lawyer may think he does only what he is paid to do, defend his clients, rather than the fact that he is a witness, by his own conduct, to the fairness and justice to which God calls us all and a practitioner of compassion. No matter what your occupation is, God calls you to live out your life in significant ways, guided by an extraordinary vision.

WORKING PRINCIPLES

Following are certain principles that have been helpful to me in discovering my vision and aligning my life to fulfill it:

- Make sure your vision has value, that it resonates with what you believe is God's purpose for His world and it contributes positively to the lives of others.
- Present a vision of what your plan will achieve and define that vision in terms of its value.
- Map out a practical plan to fulfill the vision.
- Clearly define for others the reason your vision and your plan are worthy of the support you may be requesting.
- Carefully evaluate the benefits that will accrue to those for whom the plan is specifically directed as well as to the community at large.

- Consider how those working with you will find meaning and fulfillment in what you are asking them to do.

I invite you to think about what *your* plan would look like.

A NEW DAY

Once I was able to see and articulate a vision for my life that went beyond my own personal success, I was able to apply myself effectively to the tasks through which I would be able to effectively pursue that vision. The working principles I've just mentioned became the guide for both my personal life and my professional life.

In my work in fund-raising and resource development, these principles have guided my efforts and influenced the outcome of my work. In every undertaking I sought to establish a close working relationship with each individual associated with our campaigns. My first task was to help each person understand the value of what we were seeking to achieve and to show how his or her efforts would benefit those who would be served. If we were building a college or a hospital, a church or a synagogue, a school or a service center, or Salvation Army facilities, I would articulate as best I could the significant added value of what the project would make possible. I would cast a vision of a new day.

In each community the vision of a new day inspired participation and engendered the attitude that made success possible. By making the vision foremost, attention was focused on the value of what we were doing rather than the financial objectives. By placing value before means, we established a sense of participation that inspired a high level of commitment. The fact that we achieved solid success stood as testimony to the fact that people respond when given the opportunity to commit to a worthy cause on behalf of others. By creating a compelling, caring vision, we were able to achieve outcome.

FROM FAILURE TO SUCCESS

Some of the more than one hundred cities in which I worked had not had a successful major fund-raising effort in recent memory. In many of them great needs were created by economic recessions and financial depressions. Our campaigns still achieved success. I discovered that though cities differ one from another and economic conditions change for better or worse, the one constant is always human nature.

A city is made up of people. They are its true substance and the means by which all things are accomplished. Most people are motivated to give themselves and their resources to improve the future of their community. The campaigns with which I have been involved have proven this over and over again. A worthy, community-building vision inspires participation.

Before I began a campaign I would undertake a study that focused on the needs of the city. This assessment would help us birth a vision for the campaign. We would focus on the value of what we were trying to achieve and the needs that campaign success would enable us to address. The specific needs would, of course, differ from city to city. In each setting, however, I would stress the fact that we are interdependent and need one another regardless of our stations in life. In other words, we always help ourselves in the process of helping others. Each of us is made by God to be our brother's and sister's keeper.

The more we described the needs of the community and came to believe we could address them, the more a vision began to take shape and become rooted. A practical plan would be birthed. A campaign would take shape. Success would be ensured.

The power and influence of a compelling vision can be extraordinary. Vision-based leadership can result in extraordinary outcomes.

To the Reader:

Consider what I have just described as key ingredients in a successful campaign to improve the services of a community. Think about (1) how these same principles can be applied to your own extraordinary vision of your life's purpose and (2) how you can effectively realize that vision. In particular, answer the following questions:

* How can you articulate and describe your vision so others can understand it and decide to come on board? What value will the realization of your vision add to the world or your community?
* Who are the people you need to resource you in moving toward the realization of your vision? Who are the people you need on your team?
* Can you now begin to put your vision into a plan? What will it look like?

ACTION:

*Choose a Calling That Matches
Your Talents and Passions*

Each of us has a calling. The very term "calling" suggests that there is someone else calling us. As a believer in God, I believe that it is He who calls all of us to missions beyond ourselves. As He has made each of us unique, so He has called each of us to something unique, some special way in which we can use the talents, experiences, personalities, and passions He has given us to contribute to His larger purposes. Each of us has a purpose in life greater than we may realize, a purpose that will inspire us and others to reach beyond anything we have imagined and to achieve for good more than we ever thought possible.

The talents God has given each of us are assets we cannot acquire. We can develop them but not create them. They are God's gifts. They are as much a part of our DNA as our individuality. We can acquire certain skills and gain considerable knowledge because these can be taught, but our talents are an important part of our absolute uniqueness.

IN ALL OF US

All of us have talent. *All* of us. Jesus' parable of the talents has no one without a talent in it. Each of us has been given natural abilities to discover, develop, and deploy in the process of fulfilling a significant purpose. Our talents are as varied and unique as our personalities. Even among musically talented people, for example, there is no standard scale for measuring the musical talent of each one in that group. They are all musically talented in different ways. The musical talent of J. S. Bach was quite different from that of Peter Tchaikovsky, and both talents were even more different from those of Nat King Cole or Andrew Lloyd Webber. Like them, each of us has talent that is uniquely ours.

INVESTMENT CHOICES

Since we all are talented, we must make decisions about how we will use our talents. There are three ways we can invest the talents and resources God has given us. First, we can put in our time and make a living. Second, we can go above and beyond the call of duty and achieve personal success, expressed in position and remuneration. Third, we can recognize that our lives have meaning beyond ourselves and use our gifts and opportunities to serve others and honor God. I believe the third way is the only path to significance.

Our lives will ultimately reflect which way we have chosen. Fortunately, it is never too late to make a course correction. People have done so, even in their later years, and made significant contributions to the lives of others. But it's always best and wisest to start *now*! Our length of days on this earth is never a guarantee.

EARLY DAYS

My own story is the account of my struggle to find and fulfill a significant purpose of my life. I found that purpose early in life, and I have pursued it by partnering with a noble organization and helping its spiritual and humanitarian mission. As a young boy I prayed a life-changing prayer. The years that followed were the unfolding of the answer to that prayer. It was a prayer that defined my life.

Let me go back to my own story. On a cold April day in 1942, a team of horses pulled an old truck filled with family possessions through deep snow to an abandoned farmhouse. The farm was located a mile north of Backus, Minnesota. Backus had a population of 243 people with a main street three blocks long. A freight train passed through town twice a day, and the outgoing mail was hung on a hook that the engineer caught as the train passed the one-room station. The social center of town was the blacksmith's shop.

It took six hours of pulling and digging to get the truck to the abandoned house that would be home for the next twelve years. The snow was deep and the four horses had all they could do to pull the truck through the snow. It was dark when we reached the house, and a large snowdrift covered the front door. The house hadn't been lived in for many years. The farm had been abandoned by the previous owner and left to the bank for the unpaid mortgage. My father purchased the farm from the local banker who held the mortgage following the foreclosure.

When we entered the house we stepped into the long-lost past. Animals had been living in the house, and most of the windows were broken. It was totally empty. There was nothing inside. We were looking directly at the hardships and failures of the past. No electricity, no telephone, no heat or light or water. There was nothing but the shell of a house.

It was there I would live for the next twelve years—years that would prove the most important of my life. It was there I grew from an eleven-year-old boy to a man. It was there I learned the lessons that would prepare me for my life's purpose.

For the next two weeks we lived in a boardinghouse in Backus. We spent our days cleaning the old house and fixing the windows, unloading our furniture and belongings, and attempting to make the house as livable as possible. We purchased an old woodstove for cooking our meals and heating the house. It had an endless appetite for fuel. I cut a lot of wood over the next twelve years!

The local blacksmith made a double-barrel stove that we used to heat the house. It, too, had an appetite for wood. Wood became a major part of my life, and I spent what amounted to a full month each year cutting, hauling, sawing, splitting, and stacking wood. We used forty cords a year for heating and cooking. The winters were long and cold. I can remember temperatures dropping to 50 and 60 degrees below zero.

To acquire needed farm equipment and other necessities, we began attending local auctions. Those who were leaving their farms would sell their livestock, equipment, and other items used in farming. At these auctions we purchased our first horses, cows, hogs, chickens, tractors, and other necessities we needed to begin farming. We hired a local man to help us learn how to farm and work with us throughout the year. Our hired hand was also my teacher.

The first lesson he taught me was the art of milking a cow. In time our dairy herd grew to twenty-five milk cows. I would spend four hours a day sitting on a milk stool.

Chores began at 5:30 a.m. seven days a week throughout the year. There were no holidays. Every day began early and ended late. When it was dark we worked by the light of kerosene lanterns, our source of light in the barn as well as in the house.

Located on the north end of Pine Mountain Lake, the farm consisted of six hundred acres, half in timber and half in fields. It was a mile from the house to the front gate and another mile to town—all on dirt roads.

Another important lesson I learned was never to leave a gate open. Cows and horses will always find an open gate. You could spend an entire day solving the problem you created by not closing a gate. On the farm I learned the importance of discipline and responsibility.

Farming taught me to respect the laws of nature. The fields had to be plowed and the crops planted and harvested at the right times. The cows had to be fed and milked twice a day throughout the year. The horses and pigs and chickens needed care and feeding every day. The garden had to be planted and cultivated and harvested. It all had to be done at the right time and in the right way if we hoped to farm successfully. Nothing could be left to chance. Nature had to be respected.

Farming also taught me humility and perseverance. As hard as I worked, there was one thing out of my control: the weather. In many respects the weather controlled our lives. In humility I had to learn that some things were beyond my control and I simply had to persevere through setbacks.

EDUCATION

My schooling was limited by my chores on the farm. By the time I reached junior high school I had to assume more of the responsibility for running the farm. My father's health was failing and our hired man had volunteered for the war. Throughout the balance of my school life I attended less than two months a year.

My teachers understood the problems I faced and allowed me to study at home. I would do my lessons by lamplight between 2:30 and 5:30 each morning. At 5:30 I would begin the morning chores of feeding and milking the cows and cleaning the barn. This was the way I studied throughout my high school years. I ate dinner after chores at night because if I ate before I would fall asleep while milking the cows.

This was a difficult time for me, and my teachers gave me encouragement by coming to the farm on Saturdays and allowing me to take my tests by answering their questions. Knowing I was doing my best, they did their best to help me get an education. My teachers would often walk the mile from our front gate through the deep snow to tutor me.

The long dirt roads and deep snow became for me a symbol of the persistence without which my education would never have been possible. I learned that the more difficult our goals, the more appreciated are the results of our efforts. We learn to value those things for which we struggle. That may be the reason I value an education as much as I do. I've worked hard to educate myself my whole life. The truth, however, is that the most important lessons can be learned only from experience.

A PRAYER

When I was about fourteen years old I began to question why my life was so difficult. The reason I couldn't play as other children played. The reason I had to work every day from early morning till late at night. *Why,* I asked, *must my life be so difficult and the hours of work so long?* My life didn't seem to have a reason or purpose other than work and more work.

One day I shared my concerns about my life with my mother. She told me she had been praying for the answer to this question she knew I would one day ask. In response to my question she gave me the prayer that I have allowed to guide my life. She told me that if I would ask God for help I would receive the help I needed. I have already shared the prayer that was to set me on the path to significance: "Dear Father, please help me find a significant purpose for my life!" The answer to that prayer gave me the guidance I needed to discover my destiny and guide the steps of my life.

YOUR TALENTS

There are practical ways to find your path to a life of significance. One is to find out what your own special talents are. In my case, the hard work and discipline instilled in me during those early years on the farm became assets that served me well in accomplishing what I needed to in order to make my contribution. They became gifts. When as a teenager I conducted a successful fund-raising campaign on behalf of our local 4-H Club, I began to discover an ability to conduct successful fund-raising campaigns and unite people around a worthy common cause. Later, as I advised and partnered with a wide range of people, I found an affinity for mentoring.

You, too, must discover and develop your talents if you are to make the contribution to the lives of others that God is calling you to make.

YOUR PASSIONS

The other practical way to find your path to a life of significance is to be in touch with what you are passionate about. I have a passion for conducting successful campaigns and helping people share their resources for compassionate causes. It's interesting how this passion coincides so perfectly with my abilities and strengths!

I think it is probably the same for you. Why would God give someone a passion for something the person has no ability or resource to facilitate? Let's say a person has a passion for his church's inner-city mission, but he has no particular abilities or strengths to provide leadership for the actual mission. Are there other ways he can support the mission? Of course. He can do behind-the-scenes work essential to the mission's success. He can give generously to fund it, and he can invite others with means to do so. And he can faithfully pray for the mission. He can use the gifts he has to champion the mission about which he is so passionate.

I suggest you take seriously what you are passionate about and ask how you are uniquely equipped to contribute to that cause.

STEP-BY-STEP

Most discoveries are made by taking small steps in the right direction, and by taking advantage of the opportunities that come your way and the resources at your disposal. Follow your passion, know your talents, and you will discover your calling. Ask God to help you find a significant purpose for your life and then pursue that purpose step-by-step, opportunity-by-opportunity. The quest for a life of significance never ends.

To the Reader:

I have already suggested that as a first step toward discovering the significant purpose for your life, you think about what it is you do that gives God pleasure. In the chapter you've just read, I've suggested two more helpful questions:

* What are you passionate about?
* What are your talents and strengths?

There is still another question it would be helpful to ask:

* What kinds of things do you do that people seem genuinely to value? Often people who care about us can be extremely helpful in guiding us toward the qualities we have that suggest our calling.

Take some time now to think about those three questions. Write down the answers that come to you. What do they tell you about your calling?

ACTION:

Plan a Path to Achieve Your Calling

Life has taught me the importance of having a plan. A plan gives direction to our lives. It keeps our minds focused on the goals worth accomplishing.

I would like to share my own life plan with you. A life plan enabled me to set the direction for my life, regardless of the obstacles I faced. I have had a journey more difficult than most. I doubt that many have been required to struggle and deprive themselves to the extent I have. In spite of my own struggles, and possibly because of them, the plan I established during the early, tough times of my life may have saved me. Perhaps you can gain insight from this plan that may help you in your own life and work.

WRITING THE PLAN

As I wrote my life plan I thought of the prayers I had offered during the previous several years. I thought of my mother's strong faith and my father's determined guidance. I thought of the encouragement they had given me and the sacrifices they had made during our years on the farm. I thought of the lessons I had learned in the schoolroom of experience. I thought of the land on which we had lived and how it had responded to the care it received. I thought about the purpose for my life and the prayer that I hoped would help me find it when the time was right.

All this went through my mind when I put my life's plan into words on a piece of paper. That plan became the road map I would follow for the rest of my life.

This plan was written in a six-dollar-a-night room in the Blue Bird Motel on the way to Dallas, Texas. It had been a long day after saying good-bye to Mom and Dad and the farm. I did a lot of praying. I felt alone and afraid. It was my first long drive to a place I had never been. As I sat alone that first night in a small motel room, I took the pad of paper that was in the desk drawer and began to make a plan for the life I hoped to live and the significance I hoped to find. Here is the plan I wrote with nothing but the hope and faith Mom and Dad had given me.

MY LIFE'S PLAN

I am 24 years old. The date is August 30, 1955. I have left the farm to make a living, support my parents and pay off the mortgage and our other indebtedness. I know not what I will do, but somehow I will support my parents and myself. All the cattle and machinery and other possessions have been sold. I realize I am starting with nothing of material value, but I will work hard to be financially independent by 1996, forty years from now. At that time I hope to possess assets of several million dollars. Following 1996 my income will come from the management of my investments and other assets. During my working life my income will come from the following sources: a special type of management service that will include fund-raising, development, organization, promotion, and the advancement of charitable and business endeavors. In addition to the management services I render, a portion of my income will come from real-estate investments and stocks and bonds. At the end of my working life I will establish a trust fund into which I will place all of my income-producing assets. The purpose of this trust fund will be educational and will relate to training and development and the practical utilization of natural talents. The fact that I have no formal education has caused me to appreciate the value and importance of education. I will expect each recipient to contribute a portion of their required expenses as a means of demonstrating their determination to obtain an education from which they will benefit.

During the years that lie before me, I will seek to put my talents and abilities to productive use in causes relating to Christian principles, business and social ethics, and humanitarian causes. I will devote my efforts to helping men and women achieve their potential in terms of personal development and financial success. I will write and lecture for the purpose of helping others, by sharing with them the lessons I have learned from the situations I have faced and the challenges and opportunities that have strengthened my convictions and my faith in our country.

To accomplish these objectives I will need the help and prayers of the people whom I meet during the course of my life. I believe that when I am perplexed or in need, God will send me the person or the insight I need. I will continue the prayer that has guided me thus far. "Dear Father, please help me find a significant purpose for my life." At this moment I have nothing but debt and responsibility. I have no job or profession and little experience in the ways of life beyond the farm. I have only the faith that I will live a useful and meaningful life and the love and support of my parents. With your help, dear Father, this plan will become a reality and I will prove worthy of your love.

IMPLEMENTING THE PLAN

Before I became associated with the Salvation Army, I had conducted a number of fund-raising efforts for other charitable organizations and had developed my own procedure for raising money. I brought this approach to my service with the Salvation Army. In addition to my fund-raising efforts with the Army, I became involved in real estate and made investments that would enable me to fulfill the financial objective of my life plan. I realized that successfully developing a number of productive financial opportunities would enable me to give myself more freely to my charitable endeavors.

From the beginning of my association with the Salvation Army, I contributed between 10 percent and 15 percent of my gross income to each campaign. My contribution was always the first made to each campaign. In addition to the money I contributed, I gave substantially more in the form of economical services. The fees that I charged were all-inclusive, covering every expense related to the fund-raising effort. The average cost of all the campaigns I conducted was 2.9 percent of funds raised. In 1995 I gave my farm of six hundred acres and two miles of lake-frontage to the Salvation Army for a youth camp in memory of my mother and father. All the earnings from my investments will be used to fund the Jack McDowell School for Leadership Development at the Salvation Army's Evangeline Booth College in Atlanta, Georgia.

I share this to illustrate how important it is for any of us who want to find fulfilling success to have a clear purpose grounded in a workable plan and bathed in prayer. This has enabled me to overcome obstacles, even to turn them into opportunities. It has given me courage in the face of threat and hope against despair. I believe it can do the same for you.

FINDING A WORTHY CAUSE

I was well on my way to achieving my life's purpose when the last piece of the plan fell into place: a larger cause for the betterment of humanity, a cause worth investing myself in. I found the Salvation Army. A spiritually motivated organization, the Army is made up of men and women who have committed their lives to the service of humankind for the glory of God. It teaches and trains boys and girls from disadvantaged homes to become productive citizens. It ministers to the spiritual needs of people of all faiths and creeds. It rehabilitates tens of thousands of alcoholics and drug-addicted men and women each year. It is dedicated to counseling troubled and distressed children and adults. It operates community centers and boys' and girls' clubs that serve hundreds of thousands of children, teenagers, and adults; senior citizen centers and adult living facilities; welfare centers and employment services; hospitals and clinics. The Salvation Army is the first to arrive and the last to leave the scene of natural and man-made disasters.

As of this writing, the Army operates in 111 countries, spanning the globe. I believe the Salvation Army is a worthy part of God's strategy to save the world. That is why I have devoted my life and efforts to this organization and its noble mission.

So, dear reader, my advice to you is to pray daily that God

will help you find the calling for which He created you. When you know you have found that calling and it contributes to the lives of people, develop a plan to achieve it. Then find a cause or a group of people and invest yourself in that cause and those people, so that your own contribution to God's purposes will be multiplied.

To the Reader:

If you have been able to identify your calling, take the time now to write out a plan to realize it. As your experience increases and as you seek and receive more wisdom from your mentors (more on that in the coming pages), the plan will probably be refined further or even revised. The important thing is to get started now and not to be debilitated by uncertainty and procrastination.

Here is a simple approach you can utilize in constructing your plan:

- Having sought the heart and mind of God, having allowed yourself to see an extraordinary vision of your future, having identified your talents and all your resources, and having defined a calling that brings these together into one, now write a plan for the progression of your calling toward the realization of your vision.
- In constructing your plan, identify in sequence the steps you will need to take toward a workable strategy. You may even want to include general timelines.

ACTION:

*Channel Your Compassion to Groups or Causes
Where Others Will Benefit from Your Expertise*

I believe that anything worth investing your life in must be a calling that serves others or makes it possible for you to serve others. There is no true calling that serves only our own selfish interests. A calling, by its very nature as God-given, leads you beyond yourself to a larger family, the family of God. There you have your deepest identity. There your compassion is released. There you find significance.

God gave all of us talent in order to make it possible for us to find our callings, not to achieve the trappings of success. If you are successful personally, but your success has not contributed meaningfully to the lives of others, you have not realized your calling. The true significance of your life is to be measured by how you helped someone else find the God-given value of his or her life, the compassion of a child of God, and talents for the common good.

There came a time in my own life when it became clear to me that my own talent had meaning when I used it for the benefit of others. My talent in inspiring and garnering support for a worthy cause and in helping others to succeed gave a meaning to my life far greater than I could ever have imagined. This was the fulfillment of my purpose. It was what God intended for me when He created me. I believe the same goes for us all. Whatever your talent, it will find its intended purpose and its only true fulfillment when it is used well for others.

FOR THE ACCOMPLISHMENT OF OUR LIFE'S PURPOSE

I strongly believe each of us has a significant calling in life and the God-given talent to accomplish it. This does not mean, of course, that our talents make it all easy. Those who accomplish their lives' purposes do far more than rely on their natural abilities. They develop and discipline those talents. They also acquire needed knowledge and additional skills, without which their purposes are unachievable. Most important, in one way or another, they formulate plans to use their talents and accomplishments to serve others. And they work the plans as if they were on a God-given mission—which they are.

God did not create us to simply exist. He created all of us for a purpose that brings fulfillment and joy. For me personally, that fulfillment and joy have come through helping others achieve what they are capable of achieving. I have discovered that my purpose is to help others use their talents to do the best they can with what they have, where they are, at all times, for the benefit of others.

TO HELP OTHERS SUCCEED

During the years I was conducting fund-raising campaigns for the Salvation Army and other nonprofits, I would ask a particular person to serve as chairman of the campaign. I then made a commitment to him to do all within my ability to help him become a better and more successful person. To do this I carefully prepared a description of his responsibilities and discussed it with him. I also shared my best advice and the lessons I had learned from the most successful individuals with whom I had worked. I set out in some measure to help each chairman improve himself mentally, emotionally, and often spiritually.

In every case, I found the campaign chairman also made an important contribution to my own life. We both grew, and the synergy of our relationship reaped the harvest of a successful campaign.

CAUSE FINDS TALENT

Often a dormant talent is brought to life when the person possessing that talent is inspired by the vision of a worthy cause. When I became aware of how I could help others use their talents more effectively, my life was changed and became better focused.

All of us have unique personalities, talents, and opportunities. The Bible teaches that the Spirit of God bestows gifts and talents on His people. The apostle Paul specified that these gifts or talents are given for the common good (see 1 Corinthians 12:7), and he admonished Christians to put their gifts to use (see Romans 12:6–8) and not allow them to lie dormant. The message is clear: God has endowed us all with gifts and talents that we are to claim, develop, and put to use for the benefit of the larger community.

A SACRED TRUST

I believe that our talents, the potential for good they bear, and the influence they often carry are a sacred trust to be cherished. That is as true for you as it is for me. Think of the good your talents will enable you to do for others. Think of how they will increase the value of your life as you work to improve the lives of others. Think of how you can do the most good for them.

The happiest days of my own life have been those in which I used my talents and my abilities to help others help themselves. It will be the same for you. The combined impact of your commitment to a worthy purpose, the application of your talent, knowledge, and skills to that purpose, and your generosity toward others is beyond measuring.

DOING THE MOST GOOD

What you will gain in the process is deep fulfillment and confidence that will enable you to go beyond where you were and do more good than you have ever done. Each time you share a talent, you increase your understanding of the positive potential your talent possesses.

If your talent is musical, the more you make music, the more you will bring increasing benefit and enjoyment to others. If your talent is helping others in crucial or difficult times, each act of compassionate counsel will make you an even more effective helper. If your talent is team-building, the more you bond people around a worthy common cause, the better team-builder you become and the more good you do. If your talent is raising money, the more you do it for others, the greater will be your contribution to the common good. If your talent is generosity, the more you share with others, the more you teach others to share and the greater the impact of your life.

Whatever your talent, invest it where and with whom it will have the greatest benefit.

BEGIN NOW

The important point I want to make in this chapter is that this sharing of yourself to benefit others is something to start doing immediately. Your calling is now. It is not a later-in-life activity. If you make generosity a lifelong habit, you will more likely stay on track to realize your calling, and your contributions will be more lasting.

If your calling involves a career in a helping profession, your career itself is your primary opportunity to benefit others. If you work in the profit world, your calling will be forged by the integrity of your business practices, the ways you volunteer for groups and causes that help people, and the ways you come alongside those who find significance with the aid of your counsel and support.

To the Reader:

- Assess your involvement in compassionate endeavors and causes.
- Evaluate how effectively you are using your own talents to advance them.
- Decide what steps you can take to more effectively use your talents for the good of others.

SECOND KEY 2 ESSENTIAL:

Learn from Your Experiences

Your experiences are your best teachers. This is true of the positive experiences that stand out in your memory, and it is true of the painful experiences. They are the raw material of your education.

We learn from *both* our successes and our failures. We also learn from situations or persons that may seem at first to have nothing to teach us. Sometimes we face irritations that spur us to creative solutions, teaching us to value tough challenges as opportunities for significant outcomes.

Good mentors are God's gifts to those who want to learn from their experiences and set a strong course toward their calling. If you haven't done so, you will want to identify one or more mentors to help you sort through your experiences, clarify your calling, and be accountable for your journey.

The following six actions will help you see the way to benefit from your experiences and, with the help of your mentors, steer the course of your calling.

ACTION:

Build on What You Learn through Your Successes

As your life begins to find a direction toward significance, reflect on past experiences of success and accomplishment. Remember them well and build on what you learned through them. They may not have seemed spectacular at the time, but if you know you accomplished something worthwhile or unique, or if you realize you experienced an important teaching moment, treasure and build on those memories. What's more, stay alert to what you can learn from every positive experience for the rest of your life. Let your experiences be your teacher.

The purpose of education is ultimately to achieve wisdom and insight. The best learner is the person who allows experience to teach him. We achieve wisdom by combining the knowledge we have gained with the experience we have acquired.

Following are three lessons I learned from experience. They were taught in ways I would never forget.

LESSON ONE: DO IT WELL

One morning after I finished the chores, Dad asked me to set a half-mile of fence on the west side of one of our fields. There are 2,640 feet in a half-mile. Dad wanted the posts set sixteen feet apart. This meant there would be 165 posts in the fence. There would be four strands of barbed wire attached to each post, making a total of two miles of barbed wire. It took the hired man and me five days to set the posts and stretch the wire.

It was milking time on the fifth day when we finished. As I was putting the cows in the barn I saw Dad in the distance looking at the fence. A short time after he had viewed the fence he came into the barn and asked a question I will never forget: "Are you proud of the fence you have set and does it represent the best job you could have done?" He reminded me that I would see the fence each time I came home from work. Then he said something else I shall never forget. "When you look down a good fence line you should see only one post." He asked me to reset the entire fence and do it the way it should be done, even and straight. As we reset the fence I thought of what he said every time I pulled a post and dug a hole.

Little did I realize the profound influence that fence project would have on my life and the way I would conduct my business. Although it was frustrating at first to have to go back and reset the fence posts, when the job was completed I realized that I had done something I could be proud of.

LESSON TWO: BE A GOOD STEWARD

Another lesson Dad taught was the importance of taking care of your possessions regardless of what these might be. I spent a good deal of time working in the woods with an ax and saw.

Dad told me never to leave the ax or the saw in the woods overnight. It might rain and they would rust, or snow and they would be covered and lost. Most of the time I brought the ax and the saw home when the day was over and put them in the shed.

One night about eleven o'clock, after I had finished the chores and gone to bed, Dad came into my room and asked if I had put the ax and the saw in the shed. I said I had left them in the woods because I was tired when I finished working and didn't want to carry them home. He told me to light the lantern so I could find my way in the woods and to put the ax and the saw where they belonged.

It took me nearly two hours of walking through snow to where I had been working to get the ax and saw and return them to the shed. It was a lesson on the responsible care of what had been entrusted to me.

The wisdom I gained from that experience has served me well throughout my life and is one of the reasons I take so seriously whatever trust has been placed in my hands. The value of any trust is increased by the care it is given, and the manner in which we care for whatever is entrusted to us, no matter how small, gives far greater value to it. My dad taught me that success is a by-product of our stewardship of what has been entrusted to us.

LESSON THREE: ANTICIPATE THE OUTCOME

Another important lesson my father helped me learn was how to anticipate and solve a problem before it occurred. Felling a tree is a good example. Before you begin to cut the tree, you determine where you want it to fall. You control where it falls by the way you place the notch and make the cut. A good woodsman will fall a tree within a few feet of where he wants it to land.

My boyhood experience in cutting trees taught me to visualize the scope of a task before beginning. We all can gain a better understanding of what the outcome of a task will be by planning and visualizing the task beforehand. Not only will we save time and prevent unnecessary problems from occurring, but we will also utilize our energies more productively.

LIFELONG LEARNING

Life is a never-ending learning experience. Almost all circumstances give us opportunities to learn something new. The primary and most positive strength we can bring to those opportunities is the thirst for knowledge and the willingness to use that knowledge to meet challenges and solve problems. The lessons learned from these experiences are deeply engrained and stay with us throughout our lives.

Add to this the love and respect from and for the teachers God sends our way, and the power of the learning experience is at least doubled. The common truism of the student-teacher relationship states: "The student cares what the teacher knows if he knows the teacher cares." When we know the one teaching us cares about us, the lessons are seldom rejected, even when they seem harsh at the time. The major lessons Dad sought to teach me were to do my best with what I have, to take care of what has been entrusted to me, and to plan ahead. These lessons, combined with my mother's prayers, have motivated and guided my life.

To the Reader:

Begin a treasure chest of the experiences that taught you how to be successful with a particular kind of challenge and to have a sense of pride and accomplishment in what you achieved. At the same time, remember the person or persons associated with each learning experience. Most of them will be mentors; some may even be your heroes. The combination in your memory of the experience and the person will strengthen the power of that experience as one turning point in your life. And finally, ask yourself how you can keep that memory before you and not lose its positive contribution in your journey toward significance.

ACTION:

Be Alert to Valuable Lessons from Unlikely Sources

Over the years I have again and again been surprised by what I have learned from persons I underestimated and others who helped me value myself far more than I had before encountering them. I have learned both to discount my prejudices toward others and to value what I could contribute personally. These valuable lessons have often come from unlikely sources.

USING THE TEACHERS AT HAND

After twelve years the old truck was still our means of transportation and the woodstove continued to cook our meals. We did get electricity and a telephone, but we never had running water. In place of a bathroom we had an outhouse, a small wood dwelling with an open seat and a Sears & Roebuck Catalogue close at hand. Our food came from the garden and our meat from the livestock we raised. I was a good deer hunter, and that meant we had a sufficient supply of venison. There was little we bought beyond what we raised. It was good that we lived a frugal and wholesome life. The closest doctor was twenty miles away! As far as my own education was concerned, I had to use the teachers at hand.

I learned many lessons from the farmers and woodsmen who lived in our community. Most had only a few years of schooling and some none at all. But each in his own way educated himself with practical knowledge from personal experience. Theirs was the knowledge that helped them survive when the winters were long and living was tough. One of our neighbors taught me one of the most important lessons of my life, a lesson that I believe has been one of the keys to my success.

On this occasion my classroom was the barn corral, and my problem was a stubborn bull calf. I was trying to lead him into the barn. I had tied a rope around his neck and was pulling as hard as I could. He wasn't moving. In the process I was expressing my displeasure in no uncertain terms.

While I was so engaged, our neighbor happened to stop by. He sat himself on the corral fence and watched with interest as I struggled with the stubborn calf. After observing what I was attempting to do he made a very wise statement. He said I wasn't as smart or as strong as the calf, and, he noted, I wasn't making much progress in achieving my objective.

My response was less than polite, and I suggested that he prove his wisdom by getting the calf in the barn. He said he could do it without a rope and without tiring himself out in the process. So he jumped off the fence, went into the barn, and got a bucket of oats. He let the calf eat from the bucket and walked into the barn with the calf following closely behind him. He looked at me with a smile and said, "It's not what you want but what the calf wants that matters."

I have never forgotten that statement or the lesson it taught me. In fact, I learned two important lessons that day. The first lesson was that I could learn something from anyone. The second was that people (and animals) are motivated to act by what they, and not you, want. That day I learned that you can get people to take your objectives seriously if you honor theirs.

THE JOY OF HELPING OTHERS

I began to see that my life's purpose was linked to the needs and desires of others. In fact, I was to learn that it revolved around helping others. Here is the unlikely way I learned this lesson. It had to do with my high school graduation.

Even though I attended school for only two months a year, I received the Citizenship Award during the graduation ceremony. The valedictorian of the class was a boy who had not been particularly kind to me. As a result of the way he had treated me in the past, I was surprised one evening when he came to the farm while I was milking and asked if I would write his valedictory speech and coach him with its delivery. I couldn't believe what I was hearing and I asked why he had come to me. He said that I was the only classmate he knew who was able to speak in public. He knew of my achievements in the 4-H speaking contests. He knew about the awards I had won. He was asking for my help.

In spite of my anger toward him for the way he had treated me, I agreed to write his speech and coach him with its delivery. Aware of his own past actions, as we worked together on the speech he told me how ashamed he was of his unkindness toward me.

He taught me two things. He taught me that you are respected when you do your best, even when the respect is hid-

den behind jealousy. And he taught me the value of helping
even those who treat us badly. In spite of the difficulty of it, it
is the right thing to do. And you usually, in some unexpected
way, reap a harvest of respect and gratitude.

Jesus taught us to love even our enemies. He also taught
us to turn the other cheek. Many see these admonitions as
unrealistic and naive. Jesus knew better: they free us from the
always destructive cycle of hatred.

As I remember my graduation night and the boy I helped
and the immense pride of his parents, I realize how important
it was for me to write that speech. I told no one that I had
written it or taught him how it should be delivered. I gave him
the speech as a gift and asked nothing in return. That evening
was the last time I saw him. But he had taught me to hold no
grudges and withhold no help.

During my professional life I wrote speeches for hundreds
of business leaders. When I wrote them I often thought of
my graduation night and how it felt to have my words and
thoughts expressed by another person of influence. Clearly I
was being prepared to coach others in their public work.

HELPING THE HELPERS

Years later I had an unexpected opportunity to write a public
prayer and assist in its delivery. At the time I was engaged in
a large campaign for Mount Saint Michael's School for Girls
in Dallas, Texas. The campaign was to be launched at a dinner meeting to be attended by 250 businessmen of the greater
Dallas area. I had asked Mother Superior, the president of the
school, to offer the blessing. She agreed to do so.

Several days later she called and asked if I would come to
her office. When I arrived she made a statement I shall never

forget. She said that prayer and meditation had been a central part of her spiritual life. Then she said: "Jack, I need your help. I can pray to our God and the Blessed Virgin, but I need your help in offering a prayer on behalf of 250 business leaders. Not only do I need your help, I want you to write the prayer you're asking me to deliver and teach me how to express my feelings in public." I said I would be honored and that together we would share a wonderful experience.

That evening I asked God to help me by giving me the words He would have her speak as she blessed those who would be working with us. As I wrote the prayer, again I remembered and drew strength from that first time I had been asked to write publicly spoken words for someone I least expected would ask. When I gave Mother Superior her prayer, tears came into her eyes. She held my hand and said: "This is wonderful. I will not change a word. You have reached into my soul and found the thoughts that will bless our efforts."

I made arrangements with the hotel to allow us to use the banquet hall in which the dinner was to be served, so that Mother Superior could practice her prayer in the room in which it would be delivered. She had memorized the prayer and I had coached her with its delivery prior to the day we practiced in the banquet hall. I wanted to make absolutely certain that she would feel confident with her delivery, and that the microphone was adjusted for the proper volume.

When the meeting was over and I took her back to the convent, she told me that this was the only time in her life she had felt the need to ask another person to do what she had asked me to do for her.

This was the beginning of one of the most unique friendships I have ever experienced. We became spiritual partners and friends. This happened because I wrote a prayer for her, and because she asked me to do something important and unexpected.

Throughout my life I have been taught and challenged in surprising ways. My teachers have been unexpected—and as varied as an unlikely sage, a boyhood antagonist, and a nun seeking help.

To the Reader:

Think of the people in your life you may have considered unlikely teachers but who gave you wisdom you still rely upon. Think of those people for whom you have had profound regard and respect but who drew from you and affirmed a strength you had not fully claimed. Take some time to thank God for them.

Now consider someone you had not previously thought of as a person you could learn from but, upon reflection, could well teach you from his or her own wisdom and talent. Ask for the person's help.

ACTION:

Choose Good Mentors

I have discovered a miraculous truth: when we are ready to learn, a good teacher will usually appear. Or, to put it less dramatically, when we become aware of the kind of knowledge a challenge requires, we then know the kind of help required and are able to identify the person who can teach us what we need to know. When it comes to the really important things in life, we need a special kind of teacher called a *mentor*. Mentors are the people who teach us and model for us the most important lessons for living and for achieving our lives' purposes.

Mentors are usually not assigned to us, but they are always chosen by us. I think one of the reasons I have had so many mentors who have had a profound influence in shaping me is that my lack of formal education forced me to actively seek out and choose my teachers. I chose people I admired, with qualities I wanted to emulate. My mentors taught me in a way no book or classroom could have. They created for me positive learning experiences, and, most important, they helped me aim for the outcomes that are genuinely significant.

THE UNIVERSITY OF LIFE EXPERIENCE

Perhaps one of the serious limitations of formal education is that the courses of study are so prescribed. They relate so often to what the student simply is not yet ready to learn or to things not really relevant in his life. Furthermore, many teachers in institutions of learning have little or no proven success outside academia. A mentor is a teacher who shares from his actual success in life and service. He gives us the important lessons of experience.

The greatest concern I carried into my professional life was my lack of formal education. I had almost none! When I left the farm I was a stranger in a strange land. There was so much to learn. I needed a mentor. I was hungry for life knowledge. I knew I could learn only from those more experienced and wiser than I was. The more they knew, the more I felt I could learn from them. I identified them and then soaked up all I could. They were my university of life.

I discovered this university had the world's greatest faculty, and all were credentialed by experience. I could afford the tuition because it was free, and I could take as many courses as I wished. The only requirement was my thirst for knowledge and my willingness to sacrifice my time and energy to pursue it. I made the decision to attend that university for the rest of my life.

Once I learned how to select my mentors, I discovered how exciting an education could be when it dealt with real life and gave me life skills. People I considered to be among the most talented, successful, influential, knowledgeable, and respected community leaders became my mentors.

I shall never forget a comment made by one of the most successful entrepreneurs and effective community leaders I've ever known. We were on the way to a board meeting, when a charming, well-dressed young bank executive entered the elevator and spoke to him. As we left the elevator and walked to the boardroom, I said to my friend, "I imagine that's the kind of promising young man you like to have working for you."

"Not on your life," he replied. "He's got too little practical experience to go with his formal education. He needs a lot more than his degrees to be successful." In time this wise gentleman became one of my closest friends—and an important mentor to me. He helped me see beyond formal accomplishments to significant contribution. The lessons he taught me were priceless, and I still live by them.

JESUS, THE MENTOR

What would the world be like had a Palestinian Jew named Jesus not gathered around Himself twelve men whom He intensively mentored over the last three years of His life? If He had not mentored those who would carry on the legacy, how would His teaching about the kingdom of God have been ingrained, His gift of love passed on, the ethics of His lifestyle embraced?

Over the past two thousand years, mentors have played a key role where the Christian movement has kept its authenticity. As the apostle Paul mentored young Timothy, so over these centuries have Christian leaders and saints kept the church healthy and the mission vital by mentoring well the next generation. Look at the spiritual leaders and heroes you know today: they've all been mentored well.

MENTORS AND YOUR LIFE'S PURPOSE

Shortly after discovering the value of mentors, I reviewed the life plan I had recently prepared. If I was to follow this plan and fulfill its intentions, I would need the right mentors to help me. I would need the support of those who could help me find the way to realize significance. Providence was obviously on my side: my chosen profession enabled me to work closely and personally with precisely the people who could best mentor me in my chosen field. Ironically, had I pursued a college degree in my field, I probably would not have learned as well.

My mentors have been people I deeply respected. They shared themselves with me generously. The debt I owe them is more than I could ever repay. Though most have passed on, they all live on in my own imagination: my personal cheering section, each person having given me something of great value, a part of himself or herself.

MY TWO MOST IMPORTANT MENTORS

At the heart of that cheering section are my two most important mentors: Mom and Dad. To be sure, I did not choose them to be my parents. But I did choose them as mentors. During those very difficult times on the farm, what got us through was the character of my parents, their values, and their incredible self-discipline—none of which was sacrificed when our circumstances were at their lowest ebb. What I saw in them, I wanted to emulate.

It was Dad who taught me to do the best I could, with what I had, where I was, at all times. He was a hard taskmaster. His lessons were taught with such conviction and force, I did not forget them. He demanded total honesty. He taught me always to do more than was expected.

Mom was the finest person I have ever known. She taught me empathy, compassion, patience, and understanding. She showed me how to be kind and thoughtful, to look for the best in others, and to encourage generously.

I am the product of many mentors, but my parents are the two to whom I owe the deepest debt of gratitude. They mentored me to make a real difference in people's lives. They opened the door to a significant life.

To the Reader:

Who have been the most important mentors in your life? What did you learn from them? Do they know how important they have been to you? Consider telling them. And don't forget to thank God for them!

ACTION:

Find the Disguised Opportunities in Your Problems

My first great opportunity to demonstrate my ability to solve a problem came as the result of an unpleasant situation. It was an opportunity that changed my life even though it began with a very humbling and disagreeable scenario. As I describe the problem, you will see the effect of a positive solution.

From the time I was fourteen I was an active member of the 4-H Club. One of the important programs sponsored by the club was the Demonstration Program. This wonderful program gave farm boys and girls the opportunity to show what they did in their work on the farm. Most of the time these demonstrations related to problem solving that produced productive results.

For years I had been an active participant in the 4-H Speaking Contest, progressing as far as Reserve Champion in the State Speaking Contest. This experience in the Demonstration Program helped equip me to undertake a demonstration that helped to change my life.

A MUDDY MORASS

It is difficult to imagine that mud and pigs could offer a life-changing opportunity. But that's exactly what happened, and here's the way it happened. For years I wanted to go to the Minnesota State Fair but didn't have the money to cover the expenses. I knew, however, that if I could present a winning demonstration at the county fair, I could win an all-expense-paid trip to the Minnesota State Fair. There I would have the opportunity to present my demonstration in competition with other 4-H'ers at the state fair.

Our county agricultural agent encouraged me to enter the demonstration at the county fair. When I asked him for some suggestions he said to pick the most disagreeable problem I faced on the farm and find a workable solution. The more I thought about his suggestion, the more I realized I had a problem that was very disagreeable: feeding our pigs in a muddy pen.

Pigs are fed at a long, narrow trough that stays in the same place. When it rains it gets muddy around the trough and the mud often gets deep. Pigs are very aggressive when being fed and I was often knocked down when putting feed in the trough.

A MOBILE SOLUTION

To solve this problem I built a trough on skids that could be pulled by the tractor and moved from place to place. I built a storage chamber above the trough with two hinged flaps on each side that enabled me to close the trough. This made it possible to control the amount of food the pigs could eat and allow several days' worth of food to be put in the feeder at one time. The feeder could be easily moved from one area to another and kept free from mud.

For my demonstration I built a small-scale model that could be assembled as I explained its function and many benefits in a fifteen-minute speech I had written.

Thus my Multipurpose Portable Hog Feeder became the first big step in my life beyond the farm. My challenge was to take a common problem and find a practical solution and show how it worked. I learned my speech by heart and delivered it to the cows as I milked them and to the corn in the field as I cultivated it row by row. I won the Champion Demonstration at the county fair and later the Grand Champion Demonstration at the Minnesota State Fair. My prize was another all-expense-paid trip, this time to the National 4-H Club Congress and Chicago Livestock Exposition as the guest of Mr. Thomas E. Wilson, Chairman of the Wilson Packing Company.

The following year, as a result of my 4-H activities I was awarded the National Achievement Honor and an all-expense-paid trip to Washington, D.C. It was there I was given the opportunity to address members of the United States House of Representatives and Senate as a farm boy who believed in his country and pursued the opportunities it offered those who were willing to do their best.

President Truman gave me the opportunity to sit in his chair, and Conrad Hilton gave me the opportunity to stay in the presidential suite of his Mayflower Hotel. It all seemed like a miracle. I was the boy who couldn't go to school and studied by lamplight in the wee hours of the morning. Now I was given the opportunity to meet the president of the United States and speak to the members of the House of

Representatives and the Senate. This all happened because of a problem that needed a remedy . . . pigs and mud!

A MORTGAGE DUE

Another great life-changing opportunity began as a financial problem. The problem was paying off the mortgage on the 4-H building at the county fairgrounds. Our county was large in size, small in population, and very poor. During the time of the county fair the 4-H boys and girls who showed their livestock and presented demonstrations had no place to stay. Many slept in the barns with their livestock or in the hay sheds. As more 4-H'ers participated, these limited accommodations became a greater problem.

The solution was to build a 4-H Club Center with dormitories on the second floor and a kitchen and dining hall on the first floor. The 4-H'ers and their parents furnished the labor for the construction of the building, and the local banker lent us the fifteen thousand dollars required for construction materials.

All the 4-H Clubs in the county participated. To retire the mortgage, every 4-H Club in the county agreed to raise money by holding pie socials, basket socials, and barn dances. The plan didn't work! After five years we had paid only the interest on the mortgage and nothing on the principal.

The state banking examiner informed the local banker that unless payments were made on the principal, he would be required to foreclose on the building. Our county agent called an emergency meeting to determine what could be done to pay the mortgage. No one had an answer. Time was running out. Something had to be done. But what?

A PLAN THAT WORKED

The following Saturday morning as we were eating breakfast, Dad asked how the meeting had gone the previous night. I told him of our discussion and the fact that no one had an answer to the problem. The bank would be required to foreclose on the mortgage if something wasn't done very soon. Dad asked how much was still owed on the building and I told him the same amount that was borrowed five years before. He looked at me for a moment and asked, "What do you intend to do about it?" I had no answer. He said, "I'll give you the day off and show you how to pay off the mortgage."

He took a piece of paper and wrote the names of business-men in our county that he believed would help to pay off the mortgage. He told me, "These men know you and believe in you, and they know what you've accomplished in your work with the 4-H Club." Beside each name he placed an amount and said, "Ask each of these men to contribute the amount that I have placed behind his name. Tell them how the money will be used. Tell them that a plaque will be placed in the building showing the names of the donors who paid off the mortgage."

When he had finished the list he told me to put on a clean pair of pants and shirt. We got in the old truck and began our eventful journey. There were thirty-six names on the list. Saturday was the day most of the farmers and woodsmen did their shopping. That meant each of the men I was to see would be at his place of business. I was able to see every man whose name was on the list. The amount of money behind the names ranged from two hundred dollars to one thousand dollars, with the thousand dollars being placed beside the name of the banker who held the mortgage.

All except one contributed the amount Dad wrote by their names. We left the farm at 9:00 a.m. When we returned to the farm that evening at milking time, the checks in my hand totaled $17,300. Two weeks later we burned the mortgage on Awards Night at the County Fair. Every 4-H Club was represented, and the clear title to the 4-H building was presented to the county agent. Not only was the building now free from debt, but the additional funds were used to establish a Youth of the Year Scholarship Award.

A problem that had existed for five years was solved in nine hours through the cooperative efforts of thirty-six men who believed in the value of an organization that encouraged boys and girls to live for a worthy purpose.

This nine-hour experience would become the cornerstone of my professional life. My father helped me believe a problem could be solved and showed me how. As a professional, I was to spend my life inspiring tens of thousands of business and professional leaders to address community problems by supporting worthy causes. This, along with many other experiences, played an important role in preparing me for the purpose for which I had prayed. Gradually, though I did not realize it at the time, my prayer was being answered through experiences that taught me the lessons and gave me the skills I would need to fulfill a meaningful life purpose.

To the Reader:

Put your memory to work to recall experiences where you were confronted with a problem of some kind and were able to find a successful solution. What did you learn from each of these successes? How can you apply what you learned to find a solution to a current problem, a solution that would benefit others?

ACTION:

See Irritants as Invitations to Find Creative Solutions

People approach their problems in different ways. Some allow obstacles to defeat them. They wring their hands in despair. Others ignore them, hoping they'll go away on their own. Delayed response only makes solving the problem more difficult. Still others rush in too quickly, before they fully understand the situation. Their precipitous actions usually make matters worse.

THE STRATEGY OF THE OYSTER

I know another way. I call it the "strategy of the oyster." The oyster faces a problem. It's called sand. Sand in the shell—the oyster's house, if you like—is not good. It can do serious damage. It is a problem the oyster must solve. His life depends on it. His strategy for solving the problem is to secrete a chemical that over time actually transforms the problem, the gritty and dangerous irritant, into a priceless pearl. The problem, as it turns out, carries with it the possibility of a valuable outcome—*if* it is approached with an appropriate strategy (in this case, the secretion that both neutralizes the threat and produces something of beauty).

I believe a hidden pearl will emerge from almost all problems that are tackled with confidence and your best wisdom. This requires a positive attitude and a willingness to obtain wise counsel from those you trust. The more you solve problems in this way, the more your problem-solving success becomes habitual.

OPTIMISM

I cannot stress too strongly the importance of a positive attitude in reaching rewarding solutions. Optimism is the belief in an optimal outcome, the conviction that there is a pearl embedded in the irritating problem, though we may not know exactly where or what it is. The pearl may be a clear-cut solution to the problem, a better way forward in life or work, an important lesson learned, or even the realization that a long-standing strategy no longer works and is worth abandoning for one more promising.

All these are pearls worth harvesting. They are the stuff of human progress in history and are important keys to the accomplishments of successful leaders. We all, in fact, are the beneficiaries of countless irritants converted to pearls by persistent optimists.

Human progress is the outcome of irritants faced and solved. In good times and bad, they have stimulated the progress that has opened the world to greater opportunities. They have created progress by exposing the need for change. Changing times require changing solutions that result in new advances. They require a willingness to perceive situations from a different perspective. The new perspective often reveals the solution. What appears first as a troubling roadblock stimulates a shift in perspective that often reveals the solution.

FINDING THE SOLUTION

Problems I have faced have taught me lessons that changed my outlook. Solutions emerged when I gained a different perspective, a fresh approach, a new insight. One of the most challenging capital campaigns I conducted was in Fort Smith, Arkansas. At the time our planning began, Fort Chaffee was the most important economic entity in that city. The local economy revolved around this large military base. A few months before the campaign began, the federal government made the decision to close the base and use it to house the Cuban boat people who had fled the Castro regime. The closure created a severe economic depression in Fort Smith and resulted in the foreclosure of more than twenty-five hundred homes that had been abandoned by former service personnel. The chairman of our campaign was the president of First Federal Savings and Loan, which had financed only one home during the previous six months.

These were the conditions we faced in our attempt to raise funds to build a new Salvation Army community center. After three months we had raised less than half the required funds. As a result of the local depression, many of the people who had lost their jobs were turning to the Salvation Army for help. The need for the new facilities was greater than ever.

I had a long and thoughtful meeting with our chairman to seek his guidance and advice. In spite of his commitment to the Salvation Army, he could see no way we could achieve success. We concluded our meeting with a prayer asking God to show us how we could reach our goal in these circumstances.

That evening I found it difficult to sleep and asked God again. In the morning I had the answer. I decided to double the amount I had contributed. It had always been my practice to contribute 10 percent of my fee to each campaign. As an expression of my own commitment to the success of this campaign, I would increase the amount to 20 percent.

When I arrived at the office I called the chairman and said I would like to meet with him for further discussion about the campaign. When I told him what I planned to do, he said he would do the same and would ask his board members to allow him to raise the savings and loan commitment accordingly. He called a special meeting of the Salvation Army advisory board members, told them what he and the savings and loan were doing, and asked them to consider doing the same. More than 75 percent of the board members agreed to do so, and some increased their company pledges as well.

The chairman then called a special meeting of the campaign organization and told the members what he, the advisory board, and his company had done. He asked as many as he could to do the same. He said the city needed the services of the Salvation Army more than ever.

The editor of the local newspaper was a member of the campaign organization and wrote a feature story about how the members of the organization were increasing their support. The television and radio stations picked up the story. The community began to respond. When the campaign was concluded we had surpassed the goal by 18 percent.

Here the solution to the seemingly insurmountable problem lay within ourselves. We, the campaign leaders, set the pace. As financial resources were diminishing, we expanded our giving. In doing so, we encouraged others to share their compassion. As is often the case, the solution was a paradox:

ask people with less to give more. The pearl of generosity was found, hidden among us.

To the Reader:

What irritating situation have you been facing recently? You may be tempted to avoid that situation because of the unpleasantness. Let me suggest a different way to deal with it: pray for God's help in finding the pearl, the surprising solution that will emerge with His help and your openness to the unusual or least expected way forward. Trust God, and have enough confidence in yourself to pursue the solution!

ACTION:

Refuse to Accept the Mind-Set of Failure

I have found that fund-raising can be a very challenging and rewarding experience when it is done for a purpose worthy of our finest efforts. As I searched for the most productive way to advance the Salvation Army's work, I developed a plan that I followed for the next forty years. The plan was based upon success in demonstrating the honesty, integrity, and productivity of the organization. It also required the commitment of those who contributed their time and talent to its mission. These two ingredients delivered a miracle: the plan never failed. Regardless of the goal or economic conditions, every campaign exceeded its stated objective with an average goal achievement rate of 169 percent.

How was this possible? How could such success be explained? What I observed was that the spiritual power of the Salvation Army's mission inspired support seldom seen in community undertakings. I also observed an admiration and respect for dedicated officers and staff. They were committed to a compelling purpose: to lift the fallen and empower the powerless. I saw communities drawn to that mission and to the officers' commitment to it.

The components of the campaigns were the same in every city. Communities differed and economic conditions varied, but my campaign strategies were basically the same. First, I found people who genuinely cared about the needs of those less fortunate. Second, I challenged them to take action to help in a concrete way.

OVERCOMING FAILURE

My first of nearly a hundred Salvation Army campaigns followed on a failed effort. Brigadier Harry Ward, the officer who introduced me to the Salvation Army and helped me find my purpose, asked me to join him for a Salvation Army advisory board meeting in Jonesboro, Arkansas. He wanted me to conduct a capital campaign for the local Army. (At the time he didn't mention that the meeting had been called to announce the failure of the recent campaign.) He said he needed help in turning the situation around. He wanted me to inspire the members of the advisory board to reclaim and then achieve their original stated objective.

Prior to the meeting he had given me a list of the members of the board and the positions they held in the community. He wanted me to be aware that the leaders of the community were on that board and that the chairman was actually the editor of the local newspaper.

After the editor had stated the purpose of the meeting, he called on Brigadier Ward to make his introduction. As I was being introduced I was silently asking God for help. What could I say at a time like this that would inspire the board to succeed? I hadn't been briefed on what to expect, and this was my first encounter with the Salvation Army. I took a deep breath and asked God for more help. When I rose to speak, a strange feeling of confidence came over me. For some reason, I was no longer afraid.

The words came to me as if they were not my words. I began by expressing appreciation to the members of the advisory board for what they had done for the Salvation Army. I read out loud the list of names I had been given, noting the position of prominence each person held in the community. I said, "You are the leaders of this community. I can't believe what you are about to do. You have come together on this occasion to announce to the community that you have failed in your efforts to support the future of the Salvation Army's work. Knowing who you are and what you represent to the city, I don't believe you want to make this announcement. I believe there is a solution to the problem you face, and if you are willing, I will try to help you."

After further discussion they asked me to leave the room while they took a vote. In about ten minutes I was asked to return and the chairman said they would like my help in raising the money they had failed to raise. When asked what I thought was the first thing they should do, my response was for each member to double the amount he or she had previously agreed to contribute.

There was a long silence before laughter began. The ice was broken—and my life with the Salvation Army was about to begin. All but one of the members agreed to double their original contributions. Within six weeks we had reached 150 percent of the original goal.

As we were leaving the meeting, I asked Brigadier Ward

why he hadn't informed me of what I was going to face when I met the board. He said he was afraid I wouldn't join him for the meeting if I knew how desperate the situation was.

BUILDING ON SUCCESS

Shortly after this experience I received another call from Brigadier Ward, asking if I would help him with a campaign in Lafayette, Louisiana. This time he told me of the problems the advisory board faced. Twice they had engaged fundraising companies to conduct a capital campaign and twice their efforts had failed. When I asked about the reason for the failures I was told that Lafayette was predominantly Catholic and the bishop was not a supporter of the Salvation Army, a Protestant organization. In the past I had conducted several campaigns for Catholic organizations, including colleges, hospitals, churches, and schools. I had many friends in the priesthood and sisterhood and knew they supported worthy causes. At the time I received the call from Brigadier Ward, I was actively involved in another Salvation Army campaign, but I said I would go to Lafayette and meet with the advisory board as soon as possible.

That night I pondered the problem the Salvation Army faced in Lafayette. I decided to call the diocese of that city and ask for the name of the bishop and the address of the diocese office. The following morning I wrote the bishop a letter explaining the Salvation Army's needs and asking for his blessing and spiritual support.

In a few days I received a letter from the bishop stating that I would receive his blessings as well as his spiritual support. I responded immediately with an expression of gratitude and told him how much his support would be appreciated and what a positive influence it would have on our efforts. Within a week I received a second letter assuring me of his support. Attached to the letter was his personal check for $1,600 payable to the Salvation Army Capital Campaign.

I called Brigadier Ward and told him what had happened. His first words were: "I can't believe this. Nothing like this has ever happened." A feature story soon appeared in the *Catholic Register* with the headline "Bishop Gives Cash to Salvation Army." This was the beginning of the miracles that were to follow.

Within a year I was able to go to Lafayette and begin the campaign. In the meantime I had been working with the advisory board members to build their confidence in the eventual success of our efforts. The president of the First National Bank had agreed to serve as chairman of the campaign. However, he had experienced the two previous failures and needed a great deal of assurance before he would accept the chairmanship. I assured him that he would have the needed support.

Even though I had not officially arrived in Lafayette, I maintained communication with the bishop and asked if he would consider being the honorary chairman. His answer was "Yes!" When I arrived in Lafayette I met with the chairman and informed him who his honorary chairman would be. He looked at me in amazement and without a word began pacing the floor. When he spoke he said, "How in the name of God could this have happened?"

My answer was "Prayer." I told him I had asked God for help.

He responded: "You must have a direct connection with Him."

I told him I believed the campaign would succeed because it was of God and godly people were behind it. It did succeed; 150 percent of the goal was raised. The bishop spoke at the victory celebration and said that he believed the Salvation Army's campaign had done more to bring the community together than any other activity he knew of.

FINDING MY DESTINY

These early experiences with the Salvation Army left no doubt in my mind that I had found a significant purpose for my life. All that I had done before prepared me for what I would do the rest of my life. Little did I realize when I wrote my life plan that it would be realized through my work with this organization and that I would find my fulfillment by helping it carry out its mission. The more I sought to help others understand the Army's mission, the more I found my own life influenced by the positive and productive nature of its work. The more I worked with the Army's officers on a daily basis, the more I appreciated the influence of their commitment and the spiritual effect they had upon the lives of those they helped.

The Salvation Army had a mission deserving of support. But all too frequently the support needed to serve the community effectively was lacking. My mission was to turn this failure around by inviting people to be a part of something significant, something that contributed to the lives of people who needed the help of those who were blessed with far greater resources. My purpose was to marshal large-scale support for an army of salvation that brought help, healing, and hope to the community. I would seek to turn a community's disinterest into commitment. And I would do it through my own commitment to the Salvation Army, building positive relationships, and prayer.

To the Reader:

Sometimes failure is inevitable. No matter what you do, success cannot be achieved, and you then learn from that experience. The failure becomes a valuable teacher.

What makes defeat almost inevitable, however, is the *mind-set of failure*, the expectation that your efforts will probably fail. Think about some challenges you faced over recent years you were not able to solve because you had a mind-set of failure, not trusting yourself or your team to succeed. What can you learn from that experience? And how can you apply what you learned to a challenge you face today?

THIRD KEY **3** ESSENTIAL:

Acquire Habits That Build Character

There are certain personal qualities and attributes of character that are essential to living out a genuine calling. Developing them requires intentionality and practice:

- You must practice the solitude without which you become so caught up in busyness and distraction that you lose focus.
- You must acquire a spirit of tolerance, which will enable you to work with a wide range of people and not be polarizing or polarized.
- You must gain the self-confidence that comes with self-acceptance.
- You must become a person of integrity whose word and intention can be trusted.
- You must cultivate a positive spirit to defeat the insidious influence of negativism.
- You must be willing to go beyond what is expected to accomplish the extraordinary.

The following six actions are designed to help you acquire these important habits that build character.

ACTION:

Be at Home with Yourself

Go back with me to life on the farm during my growing-up years. Each year on the farm the challenges I faced increased. My father's health continued to fail and my responsibilities grew. My parents began to go south in winter because of their inability to cope with the cold weather and the hardships. During those months I was in charge of the farm. Each winter I would spend three months alone with one hundred head of livestock to care for and twenty-five cows to milk. At times I would be snowed in for weeks. Often I would take the cream to town on a sled because the drifting snow had closed the road.

THE GIFT OF SOLITUDE

I continued my education by reading the books of great philosophers, books that I purchased for $1.25 each from the Modern Library Company by mail. Some of the great philosophers' books helped me think more deeply about the meaning of life. These were the years when nature and solitude became my teachers. The lessons I learned in my solitude helped me understand my own life and the importance of accepting my strength as well as my limitations. It also nurtured my aspirations.

When you live alone for months at a time, you learn to be at home with yourself. You learn to accept your fears as well as your hopes. You learn the only life you ultimately control is your own. You learn to be responsible for yourself. You learn that happiness is a decision you make for yourself.

I firmly believe there are benefits that come from solitude when we open ourselves to the moment. We need not be lonely when we are alone if we keep our minds active with positive, meaningful thoughts that reach beyond our private concerns.

At first I found it difficult to be alone, but I knew Mom and Dad would suffer during the long winter months if they remained with me on the farm. It was better for them to be with their brothers and sisters in a warmer climate. Knowing this helped me through those many lonely days.

But the isolation, at times, was still painful. What I began to understand then, and now understand more fully, is that being alone can open the door to personal insight and understanding. Solitude is a gift.

SELF-ACCEPTANCE

As I mentioned, one of the benefits of being alone is the realization that you are the only person in the world who controls your life. You are the person you must know and understand if you hope to achieve peace of mind and happiness. You must accept and respect yourself regardless of the circumstances that surround your life. This was the important lesson I learned during the time I lived in solitude during the winter months on the farm. It was a lesson from which I have benefited throughout my life.

During my times of isolation I also formed a close relationship with God's nature. As I looked into the heavens at night and studied the stars and the rising and setting of the moon, I stood in awe of the magnitude of it. I knew God was in it. It was His handiwork, and I was part of it.

PEACE

I also came to understand how I was a part of it and needed to care for it. In my solitude I experienced a peace with the world that helped me accept myself as well as my circumstances. I believe self-acceptance is the cornerstone of mental health and the foundation of a successful life. "Know thyself," the advice of an ancient Greek philosopher, is profound wisdom. Self-acceptance is based on self-knowledge, and self-knowledge is possible only where solitude is practiced.

I have found that solitude is not a flight into fantasy but a way into God. The psalmist knew what he was talking about when he wrote, "Be still, and know that I am God" (Psalm 46:10). The gift of this solitude, ironically, is to know that we are not alone, that God is by our sides:

God is our refuge and strength,
an ever-present help in trouble.
Therefore we will not fear, though the earth give way
and the mountains fall into the heart of the sea,
though its waters roar and foam
and the mountains quake with their surging.
(PSALM 46:1–3)

The apostle Paul put it this way:

Who shall separate us from the love of Christ? Shall trouble or hardship or persecution or famine or nakedness or danger or sword? As it is written:

"For your sake we face death all day long;
we are considered as sheep to be slaughtered."

No, in all these things we are more than conquerors through him who loved us. For I am convinced that neither death nor life, neither angels nor demons, neither the present nor the future, nor any powers, neither height nor depth, nor anything else in all creation, will be able to separate us from the love of God that is in Christ Jesus our Lord.
(ROMANS 8:35–39)

In solitude we connect with God, we discover a strength we can trust, and we find the affirmation of a God who holds us in His love.

PRAYER

I have come to believe that solitude is the key to meaningful prayer. In solitude God invites us to a realistic understanding of ourselves in His presence. In the authenticity of that moment, genuine prayer is possible. With no pretension, we can express ourselves more freely and bring ourselves and our needs to Him in prayer.

Not only that, we bring the world to Him as well. Perhaps the most surprising thing about solitude with God is that because it helps us to be at peace with ourselves, it frees and invites us to be at peace with others. The solitude that brings us before God also opens us to the world and the needs of others.

Our solitude leads to the multitude. The heart of God beats for His world (see John 3:16), and when we spend time with Him, our hearts pick up the vibration.

I believe our happiness and contentment are found in our ability to accept and live peacefully with God, ourselves, and others. The only way we can learn this lesson and achieve this state is through solitude. As long as we are unable to be alone with ourselves and God, we will be controlled by the forces around us, shaped by compromise, and driven by our insecurities and fears. As difficult as it is to learn to be alone and as distractive as the world around us is, solitude is always possible for those in search of a significant life.

To the Reader:

Solitude is the soil that nurtures awareness of God, spiritual depth, self-understanding, and compassion. I invite you to enter the enriching experience of being alone, to draw near to your Creator, to become a person of depth and substance, and then to discover how wide is the love of God. If you have not yet discovered the gift of solitude, consider taking two actions:

- Set aside time each day to be alone with yourself and your God. Take time to be grateful, to count your blessings and realize the many ways in which your life has been blessed. Schedule your solitude when you can realistically eliminate all distractions and allow your mind to be at peace.
- Periodically (say, once a month or quarter) take a one-day or even a half-day retreat.

ACTION:

Learn Tolerance

Tolerance is the wisdom to understand and accept the value of all persons. It sees beyond our limited perspectives to a deeper appreciation of those who are different from us. It releases us from the bondage of prejudice. When we practice tolerance, we expand our insight and understanding. Few qualities enable us to reach our full potential more effectively or productively than the willingness to accept people we may not at first understand or like, and find a way to work with them.

ENGAGED TOLERANCE
Some misunderstand authentic tolerance. They see it as non-involvement, noninterference, live-and-let-live. Authentic tolerance is concerned and engaged. The truly tolerant live beyond themselves for the benefit of those who are different or even difficult. They share their blessings with those less blessed, their talents with those less talented, their love with those less

loved, and their help with those less secure. They also reach out to those they don't like.

This does not mean allowing others to tread upon our individuality. Nor does it require that we suffer the selfish acts of others who disagree with us. It means we hold our own while holding the others in our esteem. It means we seek ways to work together while respecting our differences. It means we take the risk of crossing the barrier of prejudice. It means we are sufficiently secure in ourselves to allow others to be who they are.

Intolerance is the attitude of those who are not secure in themselves. Insecurity breeds fear, and fear demonizes the unknown and the unlike. Tolerance, on the other hand, is the attitude of those who are secure in themselves. It breeds love, and love seeks to understand all things and all persons (see 1 Corinthians 13).

OVERCOMING DISLIKE

An early experience in my professional life taught me the value of tolerance and impressed upon me the need to understand a person before judging him. The classroom for this lesson was a board meeting at which I was presenting the plan for a major campaign. As I presented the plan, one of the board members began expressing his views on why the campaign could not succeed. Unfortunately, this was a strong member of the board who had substantial influence over the other members. The more he spoke, the more negative he became; in fact, in his closing comments he recommended that the campaign not be undertaken until the local economy had improved.

As I drove back to my office following the meeting, I

happened to notice a "For Sale" sign on a corner property that I had passed a number of times. I hadn't previously noticed the sign because it was covered by weeds. When I looked more closely, I saw that the board member who had just ruined the meeting was the owner.

The more I thought about him, the more I resented him. Unfortunately, he was a man with substantial authority in the business community. I realized that unless I could change his outlook, the campaign would not succeed. I thought about him all night and about how unfortunate it was that he served as a member of the board. Even though I had just met him, I disliked him immensely.

The following morning I called to ask if I could meet with him for the purpose of gaining his advice. As we spoke I found that though he was highly revered in the community, he was a man with very few close friends. He appreciated that I had come to ask his advice.

In the course of our conversation, I mentioned the sign I had seen on the corner property. He said it had been there for nearly a year. It was one of his many properties and would one day be sold. He explained that each year he sold only a few of his properties because he didn't want to be taxed as a real-estate developer.

I told him I was also in the real-estate business in a small way. This gave us something in common. We began discussing real estate as an investment and the importance of finding properties in the right locations. As I was leaving his office, I suggested that he put a bright new "For Sale" sign on the property so that more people would see it as they drove by. He said he would do what I suggested and see what happened. He said if the property sold in the near future, he would contribute whatever he received to the capital campaign.

When I returned to the office I wrote him a letter expressing my appreciation for his time and generous offer. Little did I realize how my attempt to move beyond my dislike for him and build a bridge would affect the success of the campaign. Within two weeks of the time he placed the new sign on the property, it sold. He proudly announced at the following board meeting that he would contribute a substantial amount to the capital campaign.

Not only did he contribute his money to the campaign, he became an active member of the organization and raised a large amount of money from his business associates. In fact, he was the major reason the campaign achieved more than 150 percent of the announced goal.

THE OTHER PERSON'S POINT OF VIEW

In the beginning I was very intolerant of this man and saw only the harm he could do to our collective efforts. I resented him for his attitude, negative outlook, and adversarial mindset. But when I made an effort to know and to understand, to find points where we *did* connect, I was able to see that he was actually a good and generous man as well as a helpful friend. I had wrongly judged and resented him before I understood him. I had allowed my intolerance to cloud my vision and obstruct my judgment.

I'm glad I was able to leave behind my fear of him as a threat and risk tolerance. Doing so made a profound difference, first in my own relationship with him and second in the success of the campaign.

Tolerance is the attitude that enables us to understand and accept the other person's point of view. I have found that life is truly fulfilling and friendships deeply rewarding for those who have this attitude. It opens the other person to share himself with you. It also opens the door to your sharing yourself with him. A bond is forged and strengthened. Misunderstanding is diminished. A way is opened for care and concern that transcend differences. I believe this kind of tolerance even helps us see others as God sees them.

BUILDING TOLERANCE FROM TOLERANCE

Tolerance is a cornerstone in the construction of a fulfilling and peaceful life. It offers us the opportunity to strengthen rather than destroy, improve rather than diminish, and create rather than demolish. It is the mortar that holds the structure of our relationships together and strengthens the bonds of friendship. It is an essential building block of true happiness.

An act of tolerance is a seed sown that will grow similar acts. In like manner, an act of intolerance will reap a harvest of intolerance. My attempts to understand someone will be a strong, even empowering invitation to that person to understand and accept me, to open dialogue and relationship, and to open us both to new options. Tolerance is the beginning of understanding the one we don't understand, the first step in reconciliation, the triumph of common ground over hostile differences. I have personally been grateful for those who accepted me though we didn't agree. They have given me the gift of tolerance.

I believe that tolerance is essential if we are to find significance. Intolerance polarizes and alienates. It saps one's strength and sours one's spirit. It diverts us from the significant things. Tolerance, on the other hand, builds bridges between us and makes us teachers of one another. It saves us from the distractions into which intolerance invariably leads us. It sets our spirits free to pursue a purpose beyond our own insecurities and fears.

To the Reader:

The intentional effort to understand and affirm those who don't accept or agree with you will result in some of the most rewarding relationships of your life. Think about someone you dislike, or simply can't understand, or are in conflict with because of some strong differences. Ask God for wisdom in building a bridge to that person. Then follow through.

ACTION:

Gain Self-Confidence

The major problems I faced at the beginning of my professional life were fear and insecurity. As a result of my limited education and the isolated living conditions on the farm where I grew up, I felt inadequate in the presence of knowledgeable and experienced people. My insecurity and sense of inadequacy, combined with my lack of experience, made it difficult for me to approach or converse with others, particularly those in positions of authority. When I was in high school I found it difficult even to stand before the twelve members of my class and recite a poem or lesson. I was uncomfortable in public settings.

AN EMBARRASSING MOMENT

When I left the farm I realized meeting and conversing with others would be a necessity if I was to achieve my life's purpose. I wanted to acquire this ability. As I said earlier, when the pupil is ready, the teacher or the teaching moment will come. Sometimes the teaching comes through embarrassing moments.

Shortly after I moved to Dallas, Texas, an acquaintance asked me to help him by attending a dance with the daughter of the woman he was dating. He was a wealthy man, as was the woman he was dating. I told him I didn't have a suit and didn't know how to dance. He said not to worry. He would let me wear one of his tailor-made suits, and the daughter of his date would teach me how to dance.

It was a difficult evening as I tried to follow the daughter's dancing instructions. After she and I had progressed through three dances and I felt emotionally exhausted, I was surprised when the mother made some complimentary comments about how well I danced and how handsome I looked in my tailor-made suit. The man who had invited me then blurted out, "He doesn't own the suit. The suit he's wearing is mine. He couldn't have afforded to be here had I not paid his way. I wanted him to be your daughter's date so you and I could be together."

I was speechless and left the table immediately. The mother followed me to the door, put her arms around me, and said, "You'll be my date for the rest of the evening."

When we returned to the table, she told the man that he could dance with her daughter, and for the rest of the evening she would dance with me. As we danced together, she told me that she would never see this man again. He had demonstrated a lack of character that was unforgivable. She then encouraged me to be true to myself and proud of who I was. "Do your best and others will respect you just as I do."

It is difficult to accept public embarrassment and ridicule, especially when we are young and inexperienced. When we understand, however, that people act in such insensitive and hurtful ways because they are themselves very insecure or even emotionally damaged, we can move on, secure in ourselves. The man's date saw the truth quickly and rejected his cruelty. Her affirmation of me in that situation was a generosity I shall never forget.

GENUINE SELF-CONFIDENCE

Self-confidence based on wealth or social position is a fragile structure that can crumble unexpectedly. Genuine self-confidence is molded by something much deeper.

Another important lesson I've learned is not to pretend to be something I'm not or know something I don't. My chosen profession placed me in close association with many astute and highly intelligent community leaders. I needed their confidence and respect. As a result of my limited education and lack of experience, I was acutely aware of my limitations. I knew, however, that I would be judged by what I said and evaluated by my responses to questions. So I learned to listen carefully, limit what I said, and seek to understand the other person's perspective. I learned not to speak beyond what I knew and not to challenge someone's view before I thought I understood it.

Once again my teachers were those with whom I worked. Most were older and more experienced, and as a result they often intimidated me. To overcome this intimidation, I learned to ask questions before *I* was asked questions. As long as I could encourage others to share their opinions and experiences, I could keep them from expecting answers I was in no position to give. In the process of asking questions, I learned from the answers I received. I soon realized that this was the best way for me to gain the education of which I had been deprived.

I sought to make every successful person I met my teacher. I learned from them all. I benefited from their experiences. The more I learned, the more secure I became. As time passed I became a teacher. What I learned I shared, and as I shared I learned more and was able to do more for those with whom I worked.

The lessons we learn from those who have achieved success are the most important, because they are based on reality, experience, and proven effectiveness. My mentors gave me the building blocks, not only of my competence, but also of my self-confidence.

Self-Acceptance

The first key to self-confidence is self-acceptance, which is genuine humility based on an honest evaluation of our strengths and weaknesses, our assets and liabilities. There is great wisdom in the Proverbs, "Pride goes before destruction, a haughty spirit before a fall" (16:18). Pride is the inflation of our egos to hide our low self-esteem. Self-acceptance is based on the knowledge that God created us as the unique persons we are: there is nothing to be ashamed of and nothing to pretend about. It is amazing how much self-confidence comes from such basic self-acceptance.

Gratitude

I found the second key to self-confidence when I discovered *gratitude*. I learned gratitude during a very difficult time in my life. The problems I faced and the fear that ensued became my teachers. One evening as I lay in bed, I tried to pray. No prayer came to me. My mind was consumed by fear, and my despondent thoughts cast a cloud of doubt over my life.

Then something happened that changed everything. I began thinking of the good things that had come to me. I gave thanks for the love of my parents and for the good health I had enjoyed since birth. I began to count my blessings, as few as these seemed to be at the time. I gave thanks for my work and for the possibility of more and better work. Gradually, the cloud of fear began to disappear, and a sense of peace came over me. I had discovered gratitude.

I began to understand how important it was to appreciate my blessings and be grateful for the good that had come my way. From that day forward, gratitude has played a major role in my life. Now, every day I focus my thoughts on the positive things in my life, and I give thanks for every blessing that comes.

When we are grateful the sun shines brighter, the breeze is softer, the world is more beautiful, and all that we do has deeper meaning. When we live in gratitude we see the best in others, as well as in ourselves. We are more optimistic, more creative, and far more positive. We overlook our limitations and focus on our strengths. When we are grateful we discover how easy it is to accept ourselves.

As I learned to accept my feelings, my thoughts, my circumstances, and myself, I realized that I had been given a wonderful life. When I accepted myself for who I was, my blessings became obvious and new dimensions opened up for me. The greatest gift was the significant purpose for which I was born, the mission of my life. It is true for all of us. Accepting ourselves and finding our life's focus open the doors of our future. This is how we receive the life God has given us.

Be grateful for who you are. Give thanks for what you have. Look for the good in others and think of what you can do to make their lives better. Be thankful for your many blessings. See who you are and who you can become. Accept what has been and know that it need no longer limit you. You have every reason to be grateful, every reason to be confident.

To the Reader:

Self-confidence is the fruit of self-acceptance and gratefulness. Learn to accept yourself and to practice gratitude. Begin by doing two things:

* See yourself through the eyes of God—as His absolutely unique creation, as the son or daughter He adores, as someone born for significance.
* Express daily your gratitude to Him, as well as to individuals who have contributed significantly to your life.

ACTION:

Practice Integrity

During the almost forty years I have been associated with the Salvation Army, I've come to respect the honesty and integrity of its officers (ordained ministers). They, along with the soldiers (members), employees, and volunteers, are responsible for its reputation and the esteem in which its work is held. They have committed their lives to the purpose for which the Salvation Army was founded. Much of their strength comes from the spiritual covenant they have entered and their commitment to the Salvation Army's mission. Those who are married serve as equal partners in that mission. Between spouses there is a blending of human and spiritual love, mind and soul.

LEADERS WHO MODEL THE ORGANIZATION'S PURPOSE

This shared ministry often creates a synergy that enhances capability and concentrates spiritual purpose. When men and women bind themselves together in their work and share the responsibilities of that work, they can become a powerful team for the good of humanity. Utilizing their respective gifts, they increase one another's effectiveness. These officers are the life and strength of the Salvation Army. Not all are married and some will never marry, but their life purpose and mission are the same: the service of humankind for the glory of God.

I can think of a number of Salvation Army officers who have had a positive influence on my own life. We shared our faith as we worked together. I drew from their examples. I learned from their leadership. They were role models to many who needed them. For many children, the officer has been the finest role model they have ever emulated, the parent the children needed but never had, the teacher of lessons that would not otherwise have been learned, the friend when there was none other to give love and understanding. Ours is a better world because of these dedicated men and women and the contribution they make wherever they serve. More than 111 countries throughout the world benefit every day from the dedicated efforts of these officers. This is a one-of-a-kind organization for which we can thank God. For more than 140 years its mission of compassion has been the same.

INTEGRITY

When anyone is asked for a charitable contribution, the integrity of the organization is paramount and the responsibility of maintaining that integrity is critical. I thought of this each time I encouraged a person or company to support the Army's work. I often thought of how fortunate I was to represent an organization in which I had complete faith and complete confidence.

Organizational integrity is founded on two key principles.

The first is that the organization is clear and transparent about its mission and evaluates itself in light of mission effectiveness. The second is that it uses its resources responsibly and has strict procedures of accountability.

My extensive experience with the Salvation Army has taught me that this organization has that kind of integrity. Its mission to serve Christ by sharing compassion and hope, primarily with the marginalized, is validated again and again by changed lives, reconciled families, and new possibilities for the future. The mission is clear, uncompromised—and it is working.

ACCOUNTABILITY

I have also observed the second principle at work in the Army. No organization has stricter accountability and delivers better value for the dollar of support. The Salvation Army knows how to get return on investment. My experience in the investment world teaches me that when money is well invested, it will increase in value over time. The more intimately I became associated with the Salvation Army, the more I saw how carefully and thoughtfully it used its resources for the mission.

Officers are personally accountable for the money the Salvation Army receives in their community. Every month they are required to make a financial accounting to the members of their advisory boards, as well as their divisional headquarters. The Army's fiscal integrity is the result of its wise investment of resources, its accountability system, and its careful supervision.

It is clear to me why the Salvation Army exists. My experience with the organization teaches me that it knows its mission, regularly assesses its mission's effectiveness, uses its resources in a prudent way, and practices a transparent accountability.

I call this organizational integrity. My hat goes off to the countless personnel of the Army who give their best to this mission of compassion and regularly give account of their stewardship.

PERSONAL INTEGRITY

The integrity of an organization, however, is built on the integrity of its personnel. The Salvation Army's focus on its mission and its strict accountability to those who support it are the harvest of the people who built the organization and those who now serve in it. People of integrity are straightforward, uncompromising, and honest. They mean what they say and say what they mean. (The word *integrity* comes from the word *integer*, which is a number that cannot be divided.) Integrity is what the great Danish philosopher Kierkegaard called "purity of heart," which he defined as "to will one thing." It is the opposite of duplicity.

Many see duplicity as necessary for survival as well as success in today's world. You must play the angles, put on different faces in different places, keep your cards close to your chest, lie if need be.

Integrity is the courage to play straight, to refuse to twist the truth for your own advantage, to be fair, to be your authentic self. With integrity you can acquire the clarity of focus and the purity of life that will lead you to a worthy purpose, a life of significance.

To the Reader:

Just as the integrity of an organization revolves around the strength of its accountability for mission focus and fiscal responsibility, so the integrity of an individual revolves around accountability for the stated direction of his life and the use of his talents and resources for that purpose. For someone to say that the purpose of his life is such-and-such and then to work for other less-worthy purposes is to betray duplicity.

Perhaps the best way to assess your own integrity is to have a personal mentor or guide who will ask you tough questions and hold you accountable for living your life consistently with your calling. Consider whom you might ask to be that honest and, if necessary, caringly confrontational with you. Ask that person to hold you accountable on a regular basis.

ACTION:

Get an Attitude!

Each time we began a capital campaign I would tell those who joined our team they were becoming partners with the Salvation Army in the mission of helping others help themselves. They were becoming partners in a project that would make their community a better place. Though some of the people they were helping might live within a few blocks of their own homes, seldom, if ever, would they meet them. They would now, however, have the opportunity to touch their lives. The Salvation Army would be the helping hands of their compassion. The Army would give them the opportunity to expand the reach of their good works on behalf of the less fortunate.

CHANGING ATTITUDE

Our purpose was more than raising money. It was to bring positive change by changing attitude. We were involved in a life-altering experience for each person who participated. The

Salvation Army already understood that the key to its helping ministry was to persuade those who were in difficult circumstances to accept responsibility for their futures and believe that they could turn their situations, and in some cases, their lives around. When the attitude became positive and hopeful, help could be truly productive.

By the same token, when community leaders and board members changed their attitudes about their capacity to do the most good and make a positive difference in their community, they became empowered in a new way.

It may sound strange to say that the people who already had the most power and influence in the community were empowered. The explanation is simple. By using their capacity to put their resources to work for those who had insufficient resources to meet their life challenges and build a future, these leaders were expanding the effectiveness of their influence to bring positive change. Their empowering of others was also self-empowering. They were releasing the power of compassion, and in the process they discovered the greatest power of all, the only kind that can finally save the world.

The first reason our efforts achieved remarkable results was this change in attitude. Once key people came to believe they could make a real difference by mobilizing their resources to build a community of caring, other challenges could then be realistically met. One of those challenges was the enlistment of key leaders who had profile, influence, and resources and who believed in our cause. They would give the campaign their full support and lead the way for others. They would invest their credibility and capital in compassion.

FINDING LEADERS

In one southern city in which The Salvation Army was planning to conduct a campaign, the YMCA and YWCA had been involved in a combined campaign that had been under way for four years without achieving success. It was a very difficult time for fund-raising, and we would be attempting to raise more money than had ever been raised in that city.

When we began planning for the campaign the Salvation Army's advisory board had limited resources and influence. It was a board of dedicated individuals who cared about their community and the Salvation Army. In the beginning the obstacles we faced seemed insurmountable. I knew there was a way forward, and there were people in Charleston who could help us find it.

After discussing the Army's needs and the difficult situation we faced, I asked each board member to pray that God would open our eyes to the answer we were seeking. I asked each one to make a list of the people they felt were the most respected, influential, and affluent members of the community. Within a week we received the lists. Interestingly, the board itself had put only one of its own members on the list.

OVERCOMING DOUBT

One of my convictions is that all things are possible for those who believe. My task was to inspire belief before we attempted to begin. At the next board meeting I used my own life as an example of how a person with limited opportunity could become successful in achieving a significant life's purpose when he asked God for help. I suggested that we each had more influence than we realized, and I asked each member to pray that our efforts would be blessed.

We combined the names prepared by the board members into a single unduplicated list. From this list five names were chosen as potential chairmen for the campaign. We began with the first choice and made arrangements for the right people to make the request. I made it a policy to participate in the enlistment of every chairman, for this would be the individual with whom I would work most closely throughout the campaign.

After the decisions had been made concerning the potential chairman and those who would be involved in the enlistment process, we planned our strategy and set the date to meet with the man we hoped would become the chairman. Each man who served on the recruitment committee was a close friend of the potential chairman.

When we met with the potential chairman and introduced the purpose of our meeting, it was clear that he was aware of the difficulties other organizations were having with their fund-raising efforts. We were told this was not the time to undertake a fund-raising campaign, particularly one with a goal the size we were contemplating. He believed the Salvation Army was a fine organization and said he'd never heard a disparaging word said about it. However, as good as it might be, he said, facts were facts, and this wasn't the right time to prove what could be done.

I saw the odds were not in our favor. As we concluded the meeting I handed him a piece of paper and asked that he call each of the men whose names and phone numbers appeared on the paper before he made his decision. I told him that each had served as the chairman of a campaign I had conducted, and each knew from personal experience how the campaign was managed. He said he would do it, but we shouldn't be encouraged as the chances of his acceptance were slim.

A few days after our meeting, one of the men who was with us on the visit called and said he had just finished lunch with the man we had asked to be the chairman. He was encouraged by the remarks he had heard. The man had called all the men whose names were on the list. Each had encouraged him to accept the opportunity we had offered. Several told him he would regret not accepting the request.

In a few days he called and said the answer was yes and asked if I would come to his office and outline his responsibilities. This was the beginning of one of the most successful fund-raising efforts in the history of Charleston. It would change the way Charleston looked upon charitable fundraising.

THE POWER OF ATTITUDE

During the next year more was accomplished than anyone could have imagined. The Salvation Army's campaign exceeded its goal by $1,327,000. The combined YMCA-YWCA campaign was successfully completed. The United Way Campaign reached and exceeded its goal for the first time. The fund-raising efforts of the University of Charleston were more successful than ever.

Why was all of this possible? Why did all of this happen when the same people in the community were involved in the same efforts? The community hadn't changed. The people hadn't changed. The organizations hadn't changed. All were the same. The only thing that had changed was attitude!

People began to believe they could make a significant difference through their involvement with the Salvation Army and its mission. They began to understand they could capitalize on their own assets for the good of those seeking help and hope. They discovered the joy and freedom of giving. It began with a new attitude, the attitude that the seemingly impossible was possible and the conviction that our blessings are also reservoirs of compassion to be shared.

To the Reader:

A positive, confident attitude can transform a culture of failure into unexpected success and empower people to share compassion. Can you think of an experience you have had where attitude determined what the outcome would be, whether success or failure? Reflect on the turning point in that experience. What specifically happened that turned the tide one way or the other?

Is there a challenge you are facing today or in the near future in which you sense that a can-do attitude will turn the tide? What action can you take to instill such an attitude?

ACTION:

Reach Beyond the Expected

As I conducted and completed each capital campaign, I became more and more convinced that I had found the way to a significant life. I looked forward to each new day with increased anticipation and asked God to help me do my best. The more I presented the mission and purpose of the Salvation Army to those with whom I worked, the more I saw how the influence of its mission positively affected their lives. With each new undertaking I also found more ways I could help those with whom I worked, more ways to help them find significance.

HELPING A FRIEND

One campaign I conducted was in Pensacola, Florida. During the course of the campaign, I left the office each evening to work out at the local YMCA health club. On one of those occasions I was dressing after my workout. One of the men who served as a division chairman for the campaign was also dressing. He looked very depressed, and I asked him why.

He said he had been given the greatest opportunity of his life and was not in a position to accept it. He had been invited to purchase the company he worked for but didn't have the resources or credit to do so. He had spoken with his banker and was informed that his assets were insufficient to qualify for the size loan required.

I put my hand on his shoulder and said to him, "All things are possible, and often prayer opens the door." The following day I spoke to the president of his bank, who explained the reason the loan could not be made. I knew him personally, so we spoke very frankly. That evening I asked God for guidance and by morning I sensed I had the answer.

My friend was the president of the company the owner desired to sell. He had worked for the owner for more than twenty years. The owner was in his late sixties and wanted to retire. His son lived in a different city and had no interest in running the company. When I arrived at the office the following morning, I called my friend and asked if he would drop by for a visit. When he arrived I told him that I believed the best source of the purchase money was the owner himself. Who was better qualified to run the company than the president, and who could be trusted more to pay the asking price than the man who controlled its profits? I said I believed he could purchase the company at the owner's asking price over a ten-year period at 6 percent interest, making the payments on the loan from the profits of the company. The owner would be the lender and retain the title until the loan was fully paid. It would be a win-win situation for both the owner and the president.

As my friend listened he took my hand and asked: "Do you think it will work?" My answer was *yes*.

A few days later a changed man came into my office. He was filled with energy and bubbling over with joy. When he had presented the plan we discussed to the owner, tears had come into the owner's eyes and he had said, "For many years you have been like a son to me. My own son has no interest in the business to which I have dedicated most of my life. Now my business can be yours and I will be proud to have it continue in the hands of a man I admire and trust." My friend was able to pay for the company with his profits and did so in less than ten years.

OUR CAPACITY TO DO GOOD

When we commit our efforts to helping others, we discover we have an incredible capacity to do good. We expand our capacities as we reach beyond our own needs and interests. We focus our thoughts and efforts on the needs and interests of others. As I worked with the men and women who made up our campaign organizations, I realized they were the most successful people in the community and would become my teachers. They represented the best of the best. Each had proven himself by his own efforts and achievements. I gained enormously from them.

Conversely, I discovered that I could sometimes be of help to them, even the most successful of them. I had knowledge and experience I could share. This added another exciting dimension to my life. In the process of helping those who would benefit from the resources generated by the campaign, I could help those who were themselves giving time and effort to the undertaking. I could help those helping the Salvation Army.

BUILDING CONFIDENCE IN OTHERS

Another extra-mile effort took place in a city in Virginia. The chairman of the advisory board was one of three vice presidents of a local bank. He was a kind and thoughtful man and very devoted to the Salvation Army.

He had agreed to serve as campaign chairman. At first it was difficult for him to speak at our orientation meetings. He was not accustomed to speaking to large groups. I took the time to coach him in some public speaking techniques. I explained the philosophy on which our campaigns were based. We spoke extensively about the mission of the Salvation Army and of the services it offered the less fortunate. To give him more encouragement, I told him of my own humble beginnings and how I had struggled with insecurity and fear because of my limitations and lack of experience. I reminded him of his own accomplishment and success in banking and of his fulfilling family life. Gradually he gained confidence in his success and his ability to lead the campaign. The two of us worked well together.

I also brought the chairman of the bank of which he was vice president onto the capital campaign committee. This would give his boss the opportunity to see his leadership in action. Fortunately, the campaign far exceeded its goal and received a wonderful review in the local newspaper. Our advisory board chairman was thrilled with the success, but the best was yet to come. When the president of the bank retired, the chairman of its board asked our advisory board chairman to be the president. He had been very impressed with my friend's confident leadership of the campaign.

I believe that God intends for each of us to take the time and use our talents to help those who can benefit from our encouragement and support. Those with whom we share ourselves in this way often come along outside the scripting of our job. Exceptional people are able and willing to step outside the norm and contribute on a broader scale. Their jobs do not define them; they define their jobs. It is a calling beyond any circumscribed job description. They are more than performers of the expected; they are achievers of the exceptional.

I want to be clear about the extraordinary accomplishments I am referring to here. I am not speaking of the spectacular accomplishments of those who are the most successful in their respective fields: the president of the largest bank in town; the most sought-after and highest-paid lawyer; the pastor who has built the largest congregation. I am speaking, rather, of the person who exceeds expectations by going out of his way to help, mentor, and resource others. The way to significance is not by way of the spectacular. It is by way of seeing and taking opportunities to show compassion beyond what is required.

To the Reader:

What opportunities do you see in your own life to become more than someone making a living? Consider these possibilities:

- Help a friend you sense would appreciate your support. Invest more time than you normally do in the relationship by being available to him.
- In your employment, work with your supervisor and/or team to create added value to the effectiveness of your company's mission by setting approved

objectives that go beyond those listed on your job descriptions.

- Surprise your friends by giving volunteer service to a charitable cause that serves a marginalized group.
- Or come up with a different way you can reach beyond the expected.

FOURTH KEY ESSENTIAL:

Discover the Joy of Generosity

You pursue a calling because you believe God has a purpose for your life beyond personal success and prosperity. You pursue a calling for the sake of the human family He created and loves. You pursue a calling out of God-given compassion.

A calling requires a generous spirit. This generosity comes from our recognition of the undeserved good we have received and our desire to give back. It is a habit of unselfishness to be cultivated. It is stepping outside our private universes into a larger universe of service. It is partnering with other persons who are committed to sharing themselves and their resources. It is also practicing forgiveness, the generosity that heals.

Your generosity will be your greatest source of joy. The five action steps in this section are designed to help you nurture a generous spirit and discover the joy that comes with acts of generosity.

ACTION:

Give Back

Many people have blessed my life. Over time I have come to appreciate the help and influence of the people who entered my world at crucial times and shaped my life. I was fortunate to have such individuals come along when I was in need and receptive. Let me mention three of them.

THE AFFIRMER

The first was Clem Platner, editor of our Cass County newspaper. I was fifteen at the time I won the county 4-H speaking contest. Clem Platner called my parents and told them he would like to write an article about me in the county paper. My father told him we had been snowed in for two weeks and he would have to walk a mile through snow to get to our house. He said he would do so, and a time was set for his visit.

He took a picture of me, interviewed my parents, and wrote an article about my life on the farm. It appeared on the front page of the county paper the following week.

When I won the district speaking contest he wrote another story, then followed with another when I participated in the state speaking contest. This was the beginning of a mentoring relationship that continued for the next ten years. He gave me encouragement by writing about my endeavors.

As a result of his encouragement my confidence grew, and I accepted challenges beyond what I had previously thought possible. His encouragement was the primary reason I succeeded in 4-H Club work and became the president of the Minnesota 4-H organization, was the keynote speaker at the Republican State Convention, served as national cochairman of Youth for Eisenhower, and represented the 4-H organization as its National Citizenship winner. Clem Platner came into my life during a critical period and blessed me with his affirmation and support. He helped me believe in myself.

THE DOOR OPENER

The second person who came into my life at a critical time was Brigadier Harry Ward, a Salvation Army officer and divisional commander. The time was critical because I had not yet found a purpose for my life that was significant. As I related in an earlier chapter, he entered my life by asking me to help the Salvation Army overcome a failed capital campaign. His request was humble and sincere and his manner honest and genuine. The partnership we forged was more than successful. The campaign that had previously failed was turned into a great success.

Following this campaign he asked if I would help in another community. I was not able to do so at the time but told him I would as soon as possible. Following the second campaign, which also proved successful, I told him of my prayer. I said I had been asking God for more than ten years to help me find a significant purpose for my life. He put his hand on my shoulder and said he had been asking God to lead me to the Salvation Army ever since we first met.

A strange feeling came over me as we spoke, and I told him that I was beginning to feel that my purpose just might be to use my talents to serve the Salvation Army. I said I would continue to ask for God's guidance, and if my feelings grew stronger, and his did as well, I would consider that my prayer had been answered. As time passed we formed a partnership based on love and mutual respect. This wonderful man, who combined a brilliant mind with a humble spirit, opened the door to my life's purpose.

THE INVESTMENT MENTOR

The third person that came into my life at a critical time was Harry Harkavy, a businessman and financial entrepreneur. The time was critical because I had reached a point when my investment skills would determine my ability to fulfill my life plan. Without financial resources I would be unable to contribute the funds I had committed when I outlined my long-term goals after reaching the age of sixty-five.

I met Harry Harkavy through my wife. Harry and his wife, Leona, had become friends of Peggy as a result of meeting on a cruise prior to our marriage. In one of our discussions, I told Harry of my life plan and how I desired to make a contribution of the balance of my life after the age of sixty-five.

I told him of my desire to help others and support worthy causes, particularly the education of young people who were committed to improving themselves. He said he would help me by teaching me how to invest the money I earned. From that day until he died, I entrusted to him all that I could to invest. It began with 10 percent of earnings, then 20 percent, and finally 30 percent of what my wife and I earned together. We lived frugally and saved diligently during the first twenty years of our marriage. We have followed this objective throughout our married life so that we could support worthy causes, such as my wife's interests in music and art and my interests in the Salvation Army and our church. This is the reason I have been able to endow the School for Leadership Development at the Salvation Army's Evangeline Booth College in Atlanta.

These three individuals played important roles in my life. They helped me discover and fulfill my purpose. Each of them came along at a crucial time, as though they were gifts from God. I did not seek them out. They gave freely of themselves and provided what I needed. I accepted what they offered. I responded to their generosity.

Hundreds of others have come into my life at critical times and given me the encouragement and support I needed. The fact of the matter is that there are few things of worth any of us can do alone. No man is an island. We are by nature connected and by need interdependent. We need one another. God blesses us when those who are able to help us do so.

When we do our best and ask God for the help we need, He will send, and we will discover, those who can help us. We will find that most of our prayers are answered with the help of others. That is the way it is. That is how God made us.

Who are these godsends who come our way? They are those who have themselves received generosity and are now giving back. They are fortunate recipients who understand that the opportunities and resources they have been given are gifts to be shared with others. As God blesses us with encouragers, helpers, and mentors, so we are called by Him to bless others with our generosity.

To the Reader:

Think about the ways in which others have blessed your life by taking a special interest in you or going out of their way to encourage or help you. In what ways are *you* now giving back?

ACTION:

Cultivate the Habit of Generosity

Much of your life is controlled by habits. Habits are repeated behaviors or patterns that give regularity or stability to your life. They are things you do on a consistent basis without having to constantly invest time and energy in deciding. Without habits, each day would become heavy with an accumulation of decisions to be made. Habits are your internally programmed actions.

We could prove the importance of habits with an experiment. We could live one full day by taking no action for granted and forcing ourselves to consider alternative actions at every step of the way before deciding on the next step (even in the smallest matters). We would quickly see how much less we would be able to accomplish weighed down and exhausted by too many decisions. Habits are necessary if we are to be able to give needed attention to the decisions that are more complex, decisions for which habits alone do not suffice, decisions requiring our best and most creative thinking.

GOOD AND BAD HABITS

To say that habits are a necessary part of our daily course is not, however, to say that all habits are good. If we allow our credit card charges to increase beyond our ability to pay the balance, we have developed a habit of overspending and living beyond our means. Such a habit will diminish or even destroy our financial stability. Similarly, if we have developed a habit of finding fault with others and seeing flaws where there are strengths, we have developed a habit that will undermine our ability to work effectively with people.

Such bad habits, however, can be reversed. We can develop the habit of spending realistically (within our means) and by doing so strengthen our financial stability. We can also develop the habit of seeing the best in others and affirming their strengths, thereby building more positive relationships, encouraging success, and facilitating a better work environment.

Some habits are especially important to who we are. They are habits shaped by deeply held values. They are habits that reveal character and strengthen it. The habit of transparency and openness reveals a deeply held commitment to honesty, and the consistent repetition of that behavior reinforces that character trait. Conversely, the habits of deception and deviousness reveal and reinforce traits of dishonesty and mistrust.

NURTURING GENEROSITY

Generosity is a character trait that is strengthened by habit. The more we practice generosity, the more deeply that trait becomes a part of who we are. I personally believe that generosity is essential to a deeply happy and fulfilling life—a life of significance.

As a result of growing up poor, I struggled to develop the habit of generosity. Life was very difficult and there was never enough money for necessities. The profession I chose gave me the opportunity to see the positive results of generosity and the downside of selfishness. Those who were selfish seemed to be unhappy and dissatisfied and always wanted more than they had.

I shall never forget the experience of soliciting one of the wealthiest men in the South. He was well along in his years and he was a brilliant man with a very keen mind. When we met he spoke at length of his many business interests and the properties and institutions he controlled. He had worked hard and managed his assets well. After our lengthy discussion he asked the purpose of my visit.

When I told him I was seeking his support for a worthy cause, his expression changed. I explained the mission of the organization I was representing and how it served the less fortunate of his community. When I had finished he said that my request was undoubtedly worthy and he would give it consideration, but I should not anticipate a favorable response.

A few days later I received a three-page handwritten letter from him explaining the many reasons he would be unable to support my request. In his final paragraph he said that one day he might need the help of the organization I represented because life was very uncertain. As I reread his letter I began to understand why he was lonely and unhappy with all his wealth. He had allowed the habit of acquiring wealth to control his life and reinforce his insecurity. His lust for more had shut down his enormous capacity for generosity.

In my response to his letter I explained that I understood

his concern for his own welfare and assured him that the organization I represented would care for him if he ever found himself destitute. As my acquaintance with this man continued, I became aware that he never smiled. There was never a twinkle in his eyes. He would not trust the providence of God. He would not know joy.

THE THREEFOLD HARVEST OF GENEROSITY

I believe three things about generosity. The first is that there is no real joy and no lasting fulfillment without it. I am convinced that God has given us all the capacity to be generous toward others. Whatever talents we have and whatever resources we have been fortunate enough to acquire are never intended, in God's eyes, to be kept to ourselves or hoarded. They are to be shared. When we do, we discover something essential to the purpose of our lives. We discover generosity.

The second thing I believe about generosity is that giving begets giving. Some believe that generosity is a limited capacity. Quite the opposite is true. People are energized by their own giving. They discover the joy of it and they want to give more. Doing something unselfishly for someone else taps into the best in us. We realize that this is our purpose under God. We realize that without generosity we are diminished and our lives are locked in the prisons of our self-absorption. Generosity proves so fulfilling it becomes a habit.

The third thing I believe about generosity is that it attacks and ultimately defeats the insecurity and low self-esteem that plague so many people. We hoard when we feel insecure, as did the person I referred to earlier. We also hoard when we mistakenly (and tragically) think that our material and financial resources are the important measure of our self-worth. Andrew Carnegie is primarily remembered for his generosity, not his wealth. Those who appreciate only his ability to acquire capital do not understand the man.

Generosity is a habit worth forming. Form it and you will find where true security lies, you will know deep joy, you will discover something very important about who you are and what your purpose is—and you will contribute immeasurably to the lives of others.

To the Reader:

Evaluate your own generosity by applying the principles I've just mentioned to yourself:

- Have you discovered and deployed the generous spirit that God instills in all of us?
- Have you personally found that the more you give to encourage and help others, the more you are motivated to give again?
- Have you discovered the greater sense of personal security and self-worth that comes when you share yourself and your resources?

Based on your answers to the above questions, what step(s) are you willing to take to cultivate the habit and reap the joy of generosity?

ACTION:

Share Your Success in a Wider Universe of Need

While most of my professional work was with the Salvation Army, I frequently had the opportunity to come alongside other organizations to provide help. I discovered that the same principles for success worked in every new environment in which I applied them. I also discovered that my purpose in life was larger than one organization. Though my commitment to the Salvation Army was my professional priority, I became convinced that the knowledge and skill God had enabled me to acquire should be made available to other worthy groups where there was need and I had opportunity and time.

A NEW METHODIST CHURCH

Let me give you three examples of this happening. It so happens that all took place while I was conducting a campaign for the Salvation Army. The first occurred in Fayetteville, North Carolina. Following a speaking engagement at the Fayetteville Rotary Club, I received a phone call from a young Methodist minister who had heard me at the club. He asked if he could meet with me to discuss a matter of importance.

When we met he told me of his ministry plans and his vision for a new church facility. At the time his congregation was meeting in a small building they had purchased on the outskirts of town. In the course of our conversation, I asked him about the commitment of his congregation to the project. He described the support of his members, especially the most devoted of them. Three of them were working with us in our Salvation Army campaign. I knew these men and the contribution they were making to our campaign.

The more we spoke the more I was impressed by the depth of the young minister's commitment. I sensed his need for encouragement. This was his first appointment out of seminary. He cared about his church and had a vision for its future. I affirmed his passion for his people and their growth. I said I would help him build his church and work with his congregation on weekends and evenings. I had four months remaining to complete the Army's campaign. I said I thought this would give enough time for success.

When he asked about my fee, I told him nothing in terms of money. I said, however, I would expect his total commitment and that of his congregation. My fee would be the opportunity to help him become the minister and visionary leader he was capable of being.

A few evenings later I met with his congregation and explained how I would help them build their church. I told them my services would be a gift. There would be some costs, such as printed materials, but I would try to get those donated. I asked the man who had printed the materials for our Salvation Army campaign to contribute the brochure, pledge cards, and other printed materials we would need. He agreed to do this when I told him I was contributing my services.

We formed the campaign organization and the solicitation committee. Each committee member was responsible for contacting six members' families. We held a series of orientation meetings for the church members and explained how the church would be built and how it would help to enrich the spiritual life of each member and family. We spoke of the cost and how the building could be expanded if sufficient funds were raised. I obtained the services of the Salvation Army's architect to prepare a detailed drawing of the church so the members would have an idea of what it would look like when completed.

God blessed both campaigns. Before I left Fayetteville, the Salvation Army's campaign far exceeded its goal and the young minister's new Methodist church was a guaranteed reality. Success synergized itself. It always does. Two campaigns at once did not weaken either. Success in one gave more hope for another.

AN EXPANDED EPISCOPAL CHURCH

The next example took place in Pascagoula, Mississippi. I was just beginning the Salvation Army's campaign there. My wife, Peggy, and I were attending St. John's Episcopal Church during the course of the campaign. On our first Sunday at the church, the minister greeted us as we were leaving following his sermon. When he saw we were newcomers, he asked a few questions and discovered what I had come to town to do. He exclaimed, "Thank God, you are the answer to my prayer!" When I asked how this could be, he told me of his plans for the expansion of the church. He said that perhaps with my help his dream could become a reality.

Fortunately we had just arrived and I decided it would be possible to work with him and his congregation during my entire stay. I told him what I had told the young Methodist minister: that there would be no cost other than his commitment and the commitment of the members of his congregation. I would attempt to get all of the required printed materials contributed at no cost to the church.

By the time we had completed the Army's campaign, which reached more than double its goal, we had also successfully completed the campaign for St. John's. On our final Sunday in town we celebrated the victory of the church campaign at the 11:00 a.m. service. It had also substantially exceeded the goal. Many of the same community leaders had served in both campaigns. Again, two simultaneous campaigns energized and strengthened rather than depleted each other.

A MULTIPLE-SERVICE JEWISH TEMPLE

While I was working on the Development Program of the Salvation Army's Southern Territory, I received a call from Alex Schoenbaum, the chairman of the development program. He asked if I would help his rabbi raise the funds needed to expand Temple Beth Shalom in Sarasota, Florida. I said I would, and he flew his rabbi to Atlanta to meet with me.

The first thing I asked his rabbi was to tell me of his hopes for the temple and how his hopes would enrich the life of his congregation. I soon discovered his vision was far greater than his congregation's. Sensing the depth of his commitment, I told him it would be possible to achieve his dream in spite of the resistance he had received from his membership. I asked him to divide his congregation into three groups: those between the ages of sixteen and thirty-five, those between thirty-six and sixty-five, and those above sixty-five. I then asked him to prepare a list of the social and spiritual needs he felt most affected each of the three groups.

At our second meeting we analyzed his findings and noted the number of members who fell within each age-group. I wanted to know how he felt the life of the temple could beneficially serve the specific needs of each group. Once this was done I asked him to arrange for me to speak to each group separately. I would explain how each of the projects would benefit them. Then I spoke to the entire congregation and discussed the ways everyone would benefit from their rabbi's dream. I asked all the members to think of the temple as the center of their spiritual lives and then to envision what they desired most for the temple to be.

The final plan that was approved was twice the size of the original plan that had met with resistance because of cost. The plan grew from $2,000,000 to $4,500,000 and included a family center, a youth and teen center, a senior center, a kitchen and dining hall, and a Hebrew school. We created a vision and a greater sense of purpose, and in so doing, we gave the entire congregation the opportunity to capture the rabbi's vision. I made a number of trips to Sarasota over the next six months, as the rabbi's dream became a reality. Temple Beth Shalom's membership grew in size as others captured its spirit and joined its fellowship.

These are three examples of a successful strategy shared generously. The significance of your life is enhanced when a wider range of people benefit from your success. Whatever you do well, share it with a wider world and teach others the art of doing the same.

To the Reader:

Think about your successes, no matter how small they may be. Then think about how you can share the wisdom and skills behind those successes with some person or group outside the normal course of your life or occupation.

ACTION:

*Develop Lasting Partnerships
with Those Who Share Your Vision*

The synergy of a genuine partnership is powerful. As I continued to pursue the purpose for my life, I wanted to use the abilities God had given me and the lessons I had learned to serve a greater cause. I had already raised money to support a number of worthy nonprofit organizations and would continue to do so. But in the Salvation Army I found the partnership that delivered my destiny.

FORGING A PARTNERSHIP

Go back with me to that first encounter with the Salvation Army officer who was a division commander in New Orleans. As you'll remember, in the course of our conversation I shared with him my prayer for God to reveal my life's purpose. I told him that for more than fifteen years I had offered this prayer every day and every night. He then said something that surprised me. He told me that he had been asking God to inspire me to commit my efforts to the Salvation Army. I thanked him for his confidence in me and said that I would continue to seek God's guidance. I asked that he continue to do so as well. At that time I was committed to several other projects and told him when they were finished I would consider making a long-term commitment to the Salvation Army.

Over the next few months, I thought about the Salvation Army's mission. I observed the dedication of its officers. My heart and mind began to resonate with what I saw and learned. When I had finished my commitments I called the divisional commander and asked if he felt the same as when we had last spoken. His answer was yes. I told him I also felt the same and believed that working with the Salvation Army was part of God's answer to my prayer. The hardships of my early years had both strengthened me for the challenge and helped me to understand and care for the people the Army was serving. A partnership was forged; a mutual covenant was made. I believed in the Salvation Army and had confidence I could help it achieve its mission.

As a result of the commitment I made to the Salvation Army, my life began to change. My sense of purpose was strengthened as I became convinced that tremendous opportunities to do good lay before me. I knew that the lessons of experience had prepared me for this calling. Even though I had no formal education and only limited schooling, my life experiences had been an education that no university course could ever have offered. I had completed a valuable study. I was ready to pursue my calling.

The decision I had to make was to determine if the Salvation Army would be able to give me a role through which to fulfill my life's purpose, as well as whether my contribution to the organization would help it advance its mission. I concluded that this partnership held promise.

STUDYING THE PARTNER

Once I had made a decision to work with the Salvation Army, I set out to understand the secrets of their effectiveness. I studied the Army's history from its founding by William and Catherine Booth in 1863. I learned how it operated and educated its officers and what it expected from them in terms of service. I wanted to know why it was so highly respected and the reasons there was such trust in its integrity. I wanted to know how it served humankind for the honor of God, and how its officers ministered when they left the pulpit and put their sermons into action. I wanted to understand the reasons its officers committed their lives to a work that would pay them less and demanded more from them than other churches and social service organizations demanded from their leaders. I wanted to understand why the Salvation Army had become the most respected organization of its kind in the world.

The first thing that impressed me, and something I had never found before in an organization, was the fact that its officers made a total commitment of their lives to the Salvation Army's mission. All had been educated at a Salvation Army training college and were ordained ministers. All married officers served as a team and held equal rank with their spouses.

The second thing that impressed me was the accountability required of the officers and personnel. Every local operation underwent a regular financial audit, and every local command had its own board of advisers, composed of public-spirited business, professional, and community leaders who devoted their time and effort to assisting the corps officer with the management of the Army's local operations. This was an organization with stewardship I could trust. I developed, and still have, deep respect for the Army's integrity.

COMMITTING TO THE PARTNERSHIP

A partnership was born out of which came a synergy that has delivered personal fulfillment for me and has, I hope, strengthened the Army's ability to achieve its mission. My life's purpose had found a home, a place, and a purpose that gave my life significance. My prayer was being answered. For the next forty years I was partner to an army of compassion.

All of us form partnerships of one kind or another. We do so vastly to increase the overall outcome of our efforts. Partnerships range from the friendships we have with like-minded people who share our interests and aspirations, to the more formal partnerships we enter to pursue common purposes.

Whatever the nature of your partnerships, make sure they are built on shared values and worthy objectives. Partner with those you respect and with whom your life's purpose will be best fulfilled. Partner with those who, together with you, will make a larger contribution to the lives of others.

To the Reader:

Partnerships that expand generosity are a powerful force for good in the world, and they bring greater significance to the lives of those involved in the partnerships.

- Consider how your contributions to the lives of others can be multiplied by your partnering with other persons or groups for the betterment of others.
- Determine either to improve your investment in a partnership in which you are currently involved or to create or join a new partnership that you think holds promise.
- Outline and implement the steps you are willing to take to do this.

ACTION:

Practice Forgiveness, the Generosity That Heals

Perhaps the greatest act of generosity is forgiveness. That is because the forgiver transcends his hurt and betrayal and affirms the value and worth of the offender. This is a generosity unwarranted and unmerited, which makes it all the more astonishing. It clears the air, disarming it of the stifling weight of retribution and guilt. I believe in a forgiving God, and I have been on the receiving end of forgiveness. I guess that is why I've managed, in time, to forgive those who have wronged me. I've been able to offer forgiveness only because I've been privileged to receive it.

When there has been betrayal or hurt, both sides suffer until reconciliation takes place. The betrayer suffers the guilt of his unfair actions; the betrayed suffers the guilt of his harbored ill feelings toward the betrayer. The guilt feelings on both sides are festering sores that cry out for healing. I know this from my own experience.

TWO PERSONAL LESSONS IN FORGIVENESS

Let me share two incidents from my own life when I experienced the healing, liberating power of forgiveness. In both these instances, I was the one wronged, and I was as much in need of what forgiveness would bring as the one forgiven. Both incidents occurred early in my professional life, when I was not as financially stable as I am now. One related to the default of a loan, the other to the default of a rent payment. In both cases I was attempting to help a friend.

The first involved a man who printed my campaign materials. One day he asked if I would help him get a state printing contract by lending him some of the funds he needed to purchase a larger printing press. He explained how the state printing contract would enable him to expand his printing business, and how he would repay the funds with interest over a five-year period. Within a few months after making the loan, I learned that he would be unable to repay the loan. When I asked him the reason, he said he had not used the money I loaned him to the purchase the printing press. He used it to cover his living expenses.

Over the next two years, our friendship deteriorated. I came to detest this man for his unscrupulous act of deception. My negative feelings toward him became an obsession. They plagued me day and night and grew worse with the passing of time.

The turning point came on a Sunday morning as I took Communion and asked God to help me change my negative and unforgiving feelings toward the man. As I prayed, I became convicted that I should go to him and forgive him for what he had done. When the sermon was over I called him and told him of the bad feelings I had harbored toward him and said I wanted to come in person and make peace with him.

I went directly to his home. When he opened the door his eyes were filled with tears. As he and his wife sat on the sofa, he recounted how much he had suffered for the way he had deceived me and asked for my forgiveness. I shared with him the burden my own feelings had created for me and the reason I had made the decision to forgive him and let him know face-to-face. As I stood to depart, he said he wanted to repay me in full and would do so if I would accept a five-year note payable at 8 percent interest.

Over the next five years, the note was paid in full. He became a successful salesman for a large printing company. Our friendship was restored. He regained his self-respect, and I was able to resolve my negative feelings. The forgiveness was healing—and liberating—for both of us. We remained friends until he died.

The other experience had to do with a tenant in one of my rental houses. He was a realtor who had fallen on hard times as a result of high interest rates. His sales were poor and his health was failing. He was behind a year in his rent payments and asked for additional time to fulfill his obligations to me. I granted his request. A few months passed and I heard nothing from him. When I went to the house, I found it empty. He was nowhere to be found. He had disappeared. I had been betrayed and I was bitter. In fact, I began to hate him for the way he had deceived me, especially since I had tried so hard to help him.

My feelings grew stronger and more burdensome. They started to dampen my usual more-positive outlook. Once again, I finally asked God to forgive me for the resentment that troubled my mind. I asked for help in honestly and completely forgiving this man for the way he had treated me. God again answered my prayer and released me from the burden of resentment.

Nearly two years passed from the time I had discovered the empty house to when a letter arrived from the man's wife. The letter was brief. A check was enclosed for the full amount of the unpaid rent. In her letter the wife stated that her husband had died and the life insurance settlement now enabled her to fulfill his obligation. I then understood how deeply desperate their situation had been, and I thanked God that He had freed me from the oppression of my bitterness.

THE SOURCE OF OUR SELF-WORTH

Perhaps the greatest barrier to forgiveness is the difficulty we have in separating our own sense of self-worth from the opinions or actions of others. When someone wrongs us, therefore, we feel diminished and devalued. A person's true worth, however, comes from the knowledge that he is a unique child of God created for a significant purpose, and from his own deep sense of personal affirmation and acceptance. Knowing that His followers would soon face hatred and persecution, Jesus assured them they would come through it well because of their positive worth as children of God. Therefore, He said, "no one will take away your joy" (John 16:22). In other words, those who abuse you do not define you and therefore cannot diminish you.

Hence, we must learn to separate our egos and identities from the person who wrongs us. I've learned this from my own experience. Even though helping others was the most important part of my life and work, I lived for many years with the burden of an unforgiving heart and a judgmental mind. But when I learned to forgive honestly and completely and release myself from judgment, my life changed. I asked God for help, and He gave me a forgiving spirit.

FORGIVING OURSELVES

I have also learned to share the generosity of forgiveness with myself. I know people who cannot forgive themselves. They are satisfied with nothing less than perfection in both their work and their relationships. Their failure to achieve this makes them feel perpetually inadequate and full of self-blame. When something goes wrong, they automatically feel at fault and can't forgive themselves. They live under a cloud of guilt.

For some people, forgiving oneself is far more difficult than forgiving someone else who has wronged them. The only release I know for such a person is to know and receive God's acceptance of them and His love for them no matter what. In short, their own self-forgiveness comes from God's forgiveness of them. We do not need to muster up excessive willpower to forgive ourselves. We need only to know we are numbered among the forgiven.

The more we are able to forgive ourselves, the more freedom we discover to become genuinely forgiving persons. Almost immediately following a time of forgiveness, I witness a time of peace. I have found this to be true from the first time I forgave a person who wronged me, regardless of the circumstances under which the experience has taken place. Condemnation harms the condemner as much as the condemned. Forgiveness brings a liberating joy that no one can take away. Forgiveness is an act of generosity that releases both the forgiver and the forgiven from the bondage of guilt and resentment.

To the Reader:

Be honest with yourself in answering these two questions:

- Is there some harm or injustice you've done to another person for which you need to make amends? If so, risk confessing it and asking for forgiveness. Whether or not the person responds positively, you have honored him by giving him the opportunity to share the generosity of forgiveness. You have done the humble thing. You have shown character and compassion.

- Has someone done harm to you and not asked for your forgiveness? If God leads you to do so, share your pain over the situation with the one who hurt you and offer your forgiveness. (Note: This is not always recommended, as sometimes hurtful people will use opportunities to hurt again. Pray before you do this, and seek counsel from older, wiser Christians.) Whether or not the person acknowledges any responsibility for actions that caused you hurt, you have done the right thing by sharing your feelings with him. You have practiced the generosity of forgiveness.

FIFTH KEY 5 ESSENTIAL:

Build Relationships for Life

Life is relational. As one poet put it, "No man is an island." We are a community. We need one another.

Our close relationships encourage and strengthen us. Family and friends love us and challenge us. Colleague's resource us and mentors advise us and hold us accountable. These are relationships in which we give as well as receive.

It is surprising how many people, particularly some highly successful people, have few, if any, real friends. They may have close associates with whom they are allied in a common venture for personal benefit, but these may not be true friends. Friendships, by nature, have a larger and deeper purpose than can be found in relationships built on self-aggrandizement.

Your calling is, by nature, relational. Its purpose goes beyond your success. It is built on, and it builds, strong, caring relationships. The following four actions will help you build such relationships—including a marriage!

ACTION:

Make and Keep Genuine Friends

As I write these words I am looking at the picture of a man who founded a restaurant chain. Our friendship began in a very unique way. I was conducting a Salvation Army campaign in a city in the South, and I asked his banker to arrange for me to meet with him. When I entered his office he asked why I had come. His banker had not informed him of the reason for the meeting. I said that I wanted to tell him about his local Salvation Army and what it was doing for the benefit of his community. He told me that he knew all he needed to know about the Salvation Army and wasn't in need of any further information.

REQUEST REFUSED

After we spoke for about half an hour, he asked the size of the contribution I wanted him to consider. In response I said, "Substantial." His next question was: "What do you consider 'substantial'?" I asked him, "Would you consider $250,000 to be substantial?"

Shortly thereafter I called on his closest friend, who offered to contribute $25,000, until I helped him see how he could give $250,000 at a lesser cost. He called his accountant to verify that what I was telling him was actually workable. As a result of the positive answer he received, he contributed $250,000. I sent him a letter of appreciation thanking him for the $250,000 contribution. I sent a copy of this letter to my friend with no explanation. He was impressed but did not make a contribution.

In fact, more than a year passed before I received another call from my friend. In the meantime I had become actively involved in another fund-raising effort in a distant city. When he did call me his opening statement was: "I'm ready to make that substantial contribution you've been encouraging me to make." I told him it was no longer needed because we had reached 170 percent of the campaign goal in Charleston.

He was clearly taken aback. "I can't believe you are refusing my money," he said. "This has never happened to me before." I told him that I never refuse money and I'd worked too hard to refuse his. But we had met the goal in Charleston and it wouldn't be right to accept his contribution for that campaign. However, I asked if he would make the money available when and where it was needed. He assured me he would.

LARGER REQUEST ACCEPTED

Not long afterward, I undertook the Salvation Army's largest campaign in the southern United States. It would benefit every Salvation Army corps and officer in the Southern Territory. I told my friend that the time had come for his contribution. But now I wanted more than money. He asked what I meant.

My answer was "I want *you* and your money." He responded with an interesting question: "How can I give you me?" I said I wanted him to serve as the chairman of the Salvation Army's Territorial Development Program. After I explained what was involved and the opportunity he would have to do something important for the Salvation Army, he agreed to serve. We were friends for as long as he lived.

Today, as I look at his picture on my office wall, I think of the last time we spoke before he passed away. He was a good friend and meant a lot to me. I had been happy later to help him raise the money to build his congregation's temple in Sarasota, Florida. He was a wonderful friend whom God brought into my life. I believe we enriched each other. It was a friendship built on generosity.

FRIENDSHIP IN CRITICAL TIMES

Friendships are often forged in tough times. God gives us opportunity to come alongside someone in crisis and give encouragement and confidence. During the course of a campaign I was conducting, one of the men who served as a team captain found it necessary to declare bankruptcy. Conditions beyond his control caused him to lose the company he had worked to build. He was devastated. He called to tell me he could no longer work on the campaign, nor could he fulfill the pledge he had made. I assured him that I understood and that he should not be concerned about the campaign. He needed to give full attention to his own situation.

That evening I thought of him and the tremendous burden he and his family now carried. The next morning I wrote him a letter. As I wrote I asked God to give me words that would encourage him to look beyond the present and see hope for the future. I wrote to strengthen his faith in God's providence and in his own ability to see his way through to it.

ENCOURAGEMENT REMEMBERED

More than twenty years passed before we met again. When we did, I didn't recognize him. I had just finished speaking at a Rotary Club. Following the meeting a very distinguished-looking gentleman introduced himself to me. As we shook hands I sensed something familiar about him and asked if we had met before. He reached into his pocket and took from his wallet a tattered piece of paper and handed it to me. "Yes," he said, "we've met before, and you did something that changed my life." As I unfolded the piece of paper I saw that it was the letter I had written him twenty years ago. He had taken to heart my encouragement and my confidence in him. In his crisis he had found a friend for the hour, and it made a difference for a lifetime.

HONESTY BETWEEN FRIENDS

From time to time we all have the opportunity to come alongside someone in a life-changing way. These opportunities often come to us when and where we least expect them. Sometimes they present the need for moral guidance. This happened once during a campaign in Texas. One of the newspaper publishers in the city had helped me publicize the campaign. He owned several newspapers in the state. We often had dinner together and discussed his many business interests. Most of his interests other than newspapers were related to real-estate investments and developments. He knew of my interest in real estate and would often ask my opinion or advice on what he was planning to do with his ventures.

One evening over a meal he told me of an opportunity he was excited about. I knew he had a silent partner who was the money behind most of his major endeavors. He told me that he had the opportunity to make a substantial amount of money by leaving his silent partner out of a deal. I listened as he described how he could handle the deal on his own. He was like a boy in a candy store who wanted to grab all the candy his hands could hold. When he finished he asked what I thought of his plan.

I looked at him and asked if he thought he would be doing the right thing. He said he'd thought it through and determined exactly how he could work the deal on his own. I said I was disappointed by the lack of character he would be demonstrating by the plan he had outlined. I told him he would regret what he was planning to do far more than he realized, and the price would be greater than he could imagine. He was visibly shocked by my response.

A few days later he called, and this is what he said: "You saved me from making the greatest mistake of my life. It was a setup. I was being tested to see if I could be trusted with a deal bigger than any we had ever done. I'll never be able to tell you how grateful I am that you encouraged me to do the right thing. You are more than a friend."

I believe that throughout life our moral fiber is tested. Our response determines if we are worthy of the opportunities that come our way and capable of relationships based on the highest ethical standards. I also believe that genuine friendship is possible only when friends refuse to endorse moral compromise on the part of each other. Friends make each other better.

To the Reader:

All genuine friendships are built on the foundation of proven trust, genuine respect, and unquestioned integrity. By these criteria, who are your real friends? How important are they to you? How can you strengthen those friendships?

ACTION:

If You Marry, Invest in That Person for Life

I have shared the two prayers that guided both my personal life and my professional life. I now share the prayer that answered my longing for a life partner: "Dear Father, please enable me to meet the woman with whom I can share my life's journey."

Ten years passed from the time I left the farm and set out to build the foundation of my professional life. During this time I began to consider my choice of a life partner and how I would best prepare myself for a lifelong marital relationship. My plan was to have an established profession, own a home free of debt, and be in a position to adequately support a wife, as well as my aging mother. The final payment on my home was made in June 1965. Two months later I met the woman who was to become my life partner.

THE ATTRACTION OF OPPOSITES

I had returned to my home in Little Rock, Arkansas, for five days between campaigns. During this time I received a phone call from a friend asking if I would help to host a dinner she was planning. I agreed, and at that dinner I met Peggy.

At first glance we seemed an unlikely match. Our backgrounds were very, very different. In fact, we came from two different worlds. Peggy grew up in Salzburg, Austria, possibly the most charming and genteel city in Europe. Her life had been steeped in the heritage of opera and classical music. I grew up on a farm outside Backus in a remote area of northern Minnesota. My formal education was rudimentary at best and my culture was Midwestern rural. And my taste in music, well . . .

Our personalities were also opposite. Peggy was a charmer, the life of the party, an actress seeking a stage on which to perform. With her there was never a dull moment. I, on the other hand, was comparatively shy socially, more cautious and careful about what I said and did in public. She was spontaneous; I was deliberate.

We hit it off. I guess opposites really do attract!

TWO ENTREPRENEURS

I found that she was in the business of marketing her Austrian family's candles in America. (Candle making had been her family's business in Salzburg since 1583.) She was a natural salesman with an eye for color and design. Her candles were beautiful. She was starting this business at a time in our country when women had no credit and banks would lend them no money. I encouraged her and intimated, as well, that I might be able to help her find the financial backing she needed.

I am a "fixer-upper" by nature and love to take a situation and make it better—even when I'm not asked to do so! I saw great possibilities in what Peggy was planning. She had little propensity toward the business side of things and seemed interested in my help. It was beginning to look as if, in addition to our natural attraction to each other, we also shared an interest as entrepreneurs, Peggy on the design and marketing side, I on the financial.

It was Saturday night and I was leaving for my next project the following Monday. We spent Sunday and Monday together. It was my policy to drive at night to avoid heavy traffic and save working time. On Monday evening I called to tell Peggy good-bye and say how much I had enjoyed our two days together. Quietly, I hoped she had enjoyed them as much as I had.

SPONTANEITY

What she said then floored me. It was an early expression of the spontaneity I would experience time and again during the ensuing years of our relationship. She said there would indeed be no good-bye. She was packed and ready to go with me. She intended that we get to know each other better, so she planned to visit my hometown, where we would continue to date. I picked her up at 11:00 p.m., and we drove the rest of the night. I was headed to Lafayette, Louisiana, to meet with the Salvation Army advisory board to plan the upcoming capital campaign.

As we entered Louisiana the winds grew stronger and the night darker. The highway patrol stopped us and told us we could go no farther. A hurricane was approaching. We turned west and headed for Conroe, Texas, where I was to begin a campaign the following day. In Conroe we got to know each other even better. A week later she returned to Little Rock to start her promotional campaign.

The more I got to know Peggy, the more I realized my third prayer was being answered. I had never met anyone like Peggy. She was full of creative ideas. She knew what she wanted. She was determined to succeed. But there was far more to her than hard work. She helped me see that life could also be enjoyable and full of fun.

ANSWERED PRAYER

We were married the following July. She later told me she knew she would marry me when she walked into the room and saw me for the first time. (There's that spontaneity again!) Her only questions were how and when. Her wedding dress arrived before marriage was spoken of. Her favorite designer in Paris had created a dress that could also be used for a cruise—in case I didn't go along with her marriage plans!

We began life together driving into a hurricane with trees falling and power lines crackling. It was an exciting beginning to a lifelong adventure. Until Peggy came into my life, I did nothing but work, all the time, wherever I was. She changed my life by insisting, and demonstrating, that life could include pleasure as well as a profession.

A PARTNERSHIP

Within a few years of our marriage, Peggy was producing and selling far more candles than her family ever had. When she discovered the promising market for candles in our country, we made a world tour to find where they could be produced efficiently and economically. To establish the reliable source of funding we needed, I pledged a large quantity of municipal bonds as collateral for future loans. After establishing a solid business relationship with our foreign manufacturer, we were allowed to wire funds after we received confirmation the candles were on the ship. This enabled us to avoid the need for letters of credit and the extra costs involved. This trusting relationship with our manufacturer continued for thirty years until we closed Peggy's business.

Peggy sometimes refers to me as her financial manager and consultant, and I sometimes refer to her as my best investment. We have been a partnership from the beginning of our marriage. All that we have is ours together. We have supported each other throughout our marriage. She respects what I do and the ways in which I share my life with others and for charitable causes. She understands my deep respect for, and commitment to, the Salvation Army. She has never questioned the time I so fully give to this work. We have a deep mutual appreciation for each other's interests. Peggy's interests are music, travel, history, and culture. Mine are the Salvation Army, fund-raising, development, investments, and personal service.

AN ENDURING AND EXCITING UNION

Forty years have passed since the day we exchanged our vows of marriage. During these years we have grown together in a partnership that has transcended all aspects of our lives. We have traveled to more than a hundred countries, many of which are no longer safe for travel. We have been to the North and South Poles, to the Orient and Egypt. We have walked the path that Moses trod on Mount Sinai when he received the Ten Commandments and stood where Aaron and the

Israelites worshiped the golden calf. We have visited the tombs of the Pyramids and watched glaciers calve and form icebergs. We have traveled in bark boats on the Amazon and lived with the blowgun hunters. We have slept in yurts on the Gobi Desert and climbed Ayers Rock in the center of Australia. We have walked the Great Wall of China and the path to the Temple of the Sun at Machu Picchu. Had it not been for Peggy, none of this would have taken place. She opened the doors to the world for a simple farm boy.

Peggy is also a woman of faith. Her spirituality is strong and personal. She was raised a Catholic, and I am an Episcopalian. Before we married, she said she would like to join the Episcopal Church. I told my minister of her wishes, and he arranged for the bishop of Arkansas to confirm her in a private ceremony. When we travel we attend churches throughout the world and enjoy the beauty and reverence of each sacred space. Often as I sit in silent prayer, I see Peggy in the distance lighting a candle and saying her own prayer. And I thank God for answering my third prayer in such an astounding way.

Why is our marriage so rich and fulfilling? Because we have invested so fully in it. We enjoy each other's company. We share each other's faith. When we came together in marriage, we committed for life. And we will always be with each other in sickness as well as health.

To the Reader:

If you do not have a life partner and you desire one, pray earnestly, wait patiently, and move decisively. If you are married, treasure who and what you have. Invest in keeping your relationship intimate and interesting. Intentionally grow your marriage.

If you are married, what specific actions are you and your spouse willing to take to strengthen your relationship and nurture your love?

ACTION:

*Form Partnerships That Have a
Compassionate Purpose*

Let me take you back to a capital campaign I've already described. In that particular city, we worked hard to establish the value of the Salvation Army in the minds of those who participated. As a result, a sense of purpose took shape that influenced a positive attitude toward funding that many said had never been experienced in that city before. Enthusiasm became contagious and spread throughout our campaign organization, as well as the city itself. About halfway through the campaign, I saw that we would exceed our goal.

In the same city, the YMCA-YWCA asked if there was anything I could do to help them. Many of those who had worked on this campaign were also working on our Salvation Army campaign, so I was well aware of the problems they had faced. I said that I would meet with their boards and share some thoughts that might prove helpful. I suggested that this be a combined meeting, with members of both boards in attendance.

FOR THE LARGER GOOD

When I met with the two boards I proposed a radical plan for their consideration. The plan entailed a combined facility for both the YMCA and the YWCA, located away from the center of town. This would allow for sufficient parking areas and more economical construction. I suggested that a combined board of directors be established with an executive committee composed of an equal number of members from each organization. I said that if they felt this was a positive suggestion, I would help them.

After considerable discussion by both boards, a decision was reached. They would work together and develop a plan for a combined YMCA-YWCA Community Activities Center. Shortly after this decision was made, a wonderful six-acre piece of property became available at a very reasonable price. This favorable event brought about the incentive to successfully complete the fund-raising effort on behalf of both organizations.

By the time our Salvation Army campaign had been completed, the YMCA-YWCA combined campaign was well on the way to success. The United Way campaign was soon to get under way with a great leadership team and the inspiration to achieve success. The leaders of the community had a new outlook on fund-raising that reinforced their commitment to succeed.

Strong, successful partnerships had been formed around a compelling vision of a better community. A powerful form of energy lifted the attitude of city leaders. It was exciting to be a part of it. Charleston was proving what can be accomplished when a community looks beyond its problems, captures a compassionate vision of what is possible, and partners to achieve it.

COMPASSION FIRST

It is important to recognize that capital campaigns for worthy, compassionate causes can be doomed to failure because of excessive concern over the financial objective. Money is never a worthy purpose. The value of a charitable organization is not found in the money it raises but in the help it gives and the lives it changes. Money has meaningful value to the organization only to the extent that it facilitates its compassionate purpose. This explains why so many capital campaigns on behalf of charitable organizations fail. The campaign leadership thinks its primary purpose is to raise a lot of money to help the organization survive. Such a mind-set captivates few and turns off most. Those who are in a position to provide crucial leadership to the campaign either will decline or, if they agree to serve, will do so only symbolically or halfheartedly. Furthermore, those with the financial resources to ensure that the goal is reached will give less than they are capable of giving. The campaign will likely not succeed.

The campaigns that invariably succeed are those that do two things well. First, they captivate the community with the vision of what can be done to better that community. Second, they successfully create a partnership of key leaders who are themselves captivated by the vision and have the credibility and influence to garner support. There are other key ingredients, such as an effective campaign organization and strategy, for example. But none of the other ingredients will bring success without the two essentials: a compelling, compassionate purpose and a committed partnership of key leaders who can deliver results.

I count it as one of the great blessings of my life that I have been able to work alongside some amazing people for causes that gave deeper meaning to their lives and enabled them to create new opportunities for those with limited resources. These partners became my teachers and my friends.

I pray you find partnerships as rewarding to you and as fruitful for others.

To the Reader:

Consider how you can partner with others for a cause worthy of your compassion. See that partnership in two ways:

- As an opportunity to enhance your contribution to the betterment of people's lives.
- As the forging of lifelong friendships around compassionate service.

ACTION:

Mentor Others toward Compassion

I was attracted to the Salvation Army for three reasons. The first was their mission. The second the commitment of their officers. The third, the realization that I could assist them in garnering the public support they needed to do even better what they did best.

COMPASSIONATE MENTORS

I was drawn to their mission. Again and again, the Bible teaches that a community that honors God is a community that cares for the least and the lowest. The Army's mission is to bring hope, healing, and help to the marginalized. They do this with a gospel of spiritual transformation, coaching, and practical assistance. I believe that the reason the Salvation Army is successful at helping people is that it gets involved in their lives in a personal, caring way. Most people respond to genuine compassion. I saw this compassion in action. I wanted to help.

I was also drawn to the commitment of the Army's officers.

Before I made the decision to give my time, talent, and resources to the Salvation Army, I made a thorough study of the lives and commitments of the men and women who wore its uniform. I came to see them as the sum and substance of what the Salvation Army represented. At the time I became associated with the Army, a young lieutenant out of the training college received an allowance or salary of twenty-nine dollars a week, and a major with twenty years of service received an allowance of sixty-five dollars a week. My study revealed their dedication to the mission in which they believed. I was impressed by the fact that they were willing to commit their lives to this organization. If married, both spouses held the same rank and made the same commitment. Each was required to complete the two-year officer training program. It was all or nothing. I had been associated with many wonderful and devoted people, but rarely had I seen such a level of dedication to a compassionate ministry. I wanted to help these officers succeed.

Though the officers were understandably hesitant to brag about their service or parade their dedication, I felt they still needed to be appreciated for their good work. I also felt they deserved better support from the communities in which they served. I discovered how often they were taken for granted. They were always there when their help was needed and on call seven days a week throughout the year. Day and night they were helping others. In the evenings they held classes for young people and adults, teaching them how to cope with the life challenges they faced. They were always helping those they served improve themselves and their situations.

They were teaching, training, helping, and comforting those who needed someone to take an interest in them. They fed the hungry and housed the homeless. They helped the unemployed find work and children at risk stay in school. They gave shelter to the abused and comfort to the bereaved. Yes, I was drawn to these amazing people, these compassionate servants of God, and I wanted to support them and help them do even better what they did best.

HELPING THE HELPERS

This desire became my third attraction to the Army. I came to believe that I could help them advance their mission and support their dedicated officers. I knew I could open doors to community leaders and make the general public more aware of the Army's work. I knew I could raise money. And I knew I could especially help officers manage for greater effectiveness, work with their boards more productively, and build stronger relationships with the community.

I decided to help as many people as possible understand what the Army did for their communities. I established close relationships with the editors and publishers of the newspapers in the cities in which I worked. Newspapers, television, and radio stations played a critical role in all our efforts. One of the most important meetings we would hold was an information meeting for members of the media. We sent personal invitations to each media executive requesting his or her presence, or the presence of other representatives at that meeting. The agenda was the Salvation Army's past, present, and future activities in their cities.

We would encourage as many questions as possible relating to any aspect of the Army's work. We would explain how it operated, whom it served, and the various services it rendered in that community. We would discuss the cost of its programs and how its income was generated. We explained that every dollar in the Army's budget was accounted for and every expense justified.

As often as possible these meetings were held at a Salvation Army facility. Our purpose was to bring those who were in a position to tell the Army's story as close as possible to its services and inner workings.

I also wanted to impress upon the community at large that the Salvation Army was worthy of its trust and respect. I have long believed that all charitable organizations should be held to the highest standards of integrity and expected to have an accurate and efficient means of accountability. I know of no other organization that deserves public esteem and appreciation more than the Salvation Army. Though not without its faults and failures, it is motivated by a Christian faith and commitment that will not settle for moral compromise within its ranks. It is hard on itself when it comes to ethical practice and strict accountability. Its compassionate mission cannot afford to be weakened by discrediting.

MENTORING OTHERS TOWARD COMPASSION

As I worked with the Army advisory boards and community leaders during the course of the capital campaign, I realize that my purpose was to help *them* find purpose, as well. Some of them, though good at heart, had not yet found a way to release their gifts and resources to multiply good in a community and serve others in significant ways. They had not yet learned to look beyond their own needs and the needs of their immediate families. They had not yet discovered that their purpose would not be realized until they found ways to share their gifts, abilities, and resources with those much less favored who needed a lift, a chance, a caring hand. One of my greatest joys has been the privilege of mentoring economically successful people in a life of generosity.

I believe God calls all of us to mentor others. That is how what we have learned and how we have changed can help those whose lives we have the capacity to influence and encourage. I saw my role with potential supporters of the Army to be a mentoring toward compassion. As I spoke about the needs of the marginalized and the qualifications of the Army to meet those needs, I invited the community at large and each prospect with whom I spoke to be a part of the solution. I sought to release the God-given compassion that all men and women are capable of. What I ultimately sought was for those I mentored in compassion to mentor others, and by so doing, to multiply the benefits and establish the legacy of a caring community.

To the Reader:

We vastly multiply our lives' contributions by mentoring others toward compassion. When you help someone move toward a more caring involvement in the lives of others, you are giving him or her the gift of significance. That person is discovering the most important dimension of his or her life's calling.

Who in your web of relationships can you mentor toward compassion—and greater significance? Decide how you will accomplish this.

SIXTH KEY 6 ESSENTIAL:

Don't Retire!

A life of significance is a life lived fully from now on. This includes the so-called retirement years, the years of exploring new possibilities for realizing your calling. A career ends, but a calling never does.

This last key essential invites you to see your retirement from employment as the beginning of the most rewarding phase of your calling. You can follow your vision your whole life, and your latter years allow you to share from your rich treasury of accumulated experience and wisdom.

The rest of your life is always a plan unfolding. In your senior years, you not only look back in gratitude on the way traveled, you also look forward in expectant hope to the days of your calling that still lie ahead.

The following four action steps will help you to make the retirement years your crowning investment in significance!

ACTION:

Follow Your Calling to the End

The search for my calling began as a prayer: "Dear Father, help me find a significant purpose for my life." I was fourteen when I first prayed this prayer. Now I am more than three-quarters of a century old. Over the years I've come to realize that my calling is not a profession or a position. My calling is the thread that knits my life together into a meaningful pattern that reflects my uniqueness and outlines my contributions to the lives of others. It is the guiding influence that motivates my efforts and stimulates my thoughts. It controls my attitude and governs my action. It empowers me. My calling is as much a part of my life as the air I breathe and the thoughts that occupy my mind.

A calling is a gift from God. It is given to each person who asks and who believes it will be given. It is not the profession we choose or the position we achieve. It is the outcome we seek that will give our lives lasting meaning. It goes far beyond personal achievement and personal gain. The calling God gives us is to develop our gifts and talents and direct our passion to better our world and help others achieve their callings in life.

BECOMING OUR CALLINGS

We carry our callings with us through our actions, words, and relationships. As our callings take root in our lives, we actually become their embodiment. People identify us even more by our callings than our personalities, professions, or positions:

- He is not simply the person who is quiet, thoughtful, and introspective; he is the person who is shaping ideas and plans for the benefit of others.
- She is not simply a missionary; she is the person who walks the streets of poverty, relieves suffering, and gives hope.
- He is not simply the CEO of a major corporation; he is the leader who refuses to take advantage of others, cares about his employees and their well-being, and shares his wealth generously to empower others.

At the end of life, achievement gives us only shallow satisfaction, but having lived out the purposes for which God created us brings fulfillment and peace.

LOVING OUR CALLINGS

As I reflect on my own life, I see a consistent thread woven through the fabric of my story. That thread is the incessant pursuit of my calling, and that calling has been to encourage others in achieving their potential and to support them in their efforts to do so. As I have worked hard to find positive solutions to the problems I faced, I have been privileged to help others do the same. Building on the strengths God has given me, I have been privileged to help others claim their own strengths and put them to good use.

I am convinced that what defines us, and is the final measure of our lives, is how we use our God-given callings to benefit others. As individuals, each of us is unique in terms of temperament, personality, mental capacity, energy, outlook, talent, ability, attitude, and self-confidence. Each of these characteristics has its influence upon us and upon the manner in which we respond to others. A calling, however, is the catalyst that brings these characteristics into meaningful focus and frees us to become the persons we were created to be. When we find and pursue our callings, our uniqueness becomes beautiful to see and bountiful in the harvest of our lives.

As I reflect back on my career, two things bring me deep satisfaction. One is that I discovered my calling, and the other is that I was able to put my abilities to use in making it possible for others to discover theirs. The best choices I have made were guided by those two things. As I live out my final years, that purpose and my partnerships on behalf of others will continue to motivate me and will bring me to a satisfying and rewarding completion of my life's journey.

To the Reader:

If your life is lived for a calling that benefits others, you will find that there is no real retirement. There are only successive phases in the realization of that calling. At some point in your life you may cease working for an income, but a true calling does not terminate. It simply enters the next phase, which may well prove to be the most fruitful of all.

Give some serious thought to the stages of your calling, including the stage(s) that will take place during the so-called retirement years. How do you think you will be positioned to reap the greatest harvest during those years?

ACTION:

Spend Your Last Years Sharing from the Treasury of Your Experience and Wisdom

One of the benefits of the years we live is the experience we gain. The best way to capture the value of this experience is to share it with others, and the older we become the more we have to share.

Most of us work forty years before retirement. We usually think that when we retire we can do whatever we choose. It's as if our life's purpose changes—or disappears into self-indulgence. This idea is a fairly recent development in the Western world. In fact, the isolation and segmentation of retired people, their removal from the center of meaningful interaction, consultation, and decision making, is a disgrace. It is also a substantial loss to society, which could profit greatly from the wisdom these people have gained over the years.

Fortunately, there are retired people who refuse to see their retirement years as either a mindless bliss or a demeaning curse. In fact, they refuse to accept the whole ridiculous idea of being "put out to pasture." Instead, they see their latter years as blessed with rich opportunities to make their most enduring contributions. They see open doors to sharing their wisdom, mentoring the inexperienced, and investing their resources in ways that will help others find and realize their lives' callings.

Those who refuse the idea of "retirement" are actually those who plan best for it. Those who see retirement as an ending find it hard to know how to make a new beginning. Retirement doesn't bring the deep happiness they expected to come naturally. Their lives now seem empty. Those, however, who approach and live their latter years as a time for reaping the harvest of their lives and sharing it with a larger community, find these years to be the most rewarding yet. These are also the people who, long before they retire, have a strong sense of what their latter years can become.

PLANNING A PURPOSEFUL RETIREMENT

The sooner the planning for our latter years begins, the more rewarding those years are likely to be. A fulfilling retirement is not a discontinuation but an extension of the lives we have lived and the aspirations we have nurtured. During those years we can increase the significance of our lives by proving and sharing the values we cherish. As someone whose age places him in the retirement bracket, I can witness to the continuing expansion of my calling over these latter years. My times of greatest happiness have come as a result of helping others and encouraging them to believe in their finer qualities. I have committed these latter years to doing so even more effectively.

The real pot of gold at the end of our rainbow is not material wealth to indulge us. It is something living and vibrant. It is our valuable experiences. It is gold in many forms to benefit the larger community. In retirement we have the opportunity to compound the value of this treasure by investing in the lives of others. The fact is that we greatly enhance the significance of our lives when we share our knowledge, experiences, and resources with others.

If we have found our identity only in our professions or positions, retirement weakens it at best and robs us of it at worst. But if we have found our identity in our purposes and our callings, the latter years can enhance it. When we live out our remaining years sure of whom we are and what our purpose is, we live well and we are rich where it matters most.

MENTORING YEARS

My advice, therefore, is to think about the final years of your journey well in advance. Think of the valuable contribution you can make as a mentor and the satisfaction you will receive from sharing your wisdom with others. Think of retirement as a rewarding extension of your working life. Consider the many ways you can expand the opportunities this time will offer.

As a person well into those years, I am finding these the finest and most rewarding years of my life. Reflect on what is important to you and how you can increase its value by sharing it with others. Think of your family and loved ones, your friends, your community, and what has brought you the deepest satisfaction. Think of your talents and abilities and the manner in which these can be used for the benefit of those you love and respect, as well as a host of others perhaps yet unknown to you who would be helped by your mentoring and support. You can be a guiding light and a beacon of hope for more people than you can imagine.

You can also be a compassionate friend in times of sorrow and an understanding leader for those who have lost their sense of direction. You can mentor with love and understanding, as well as guidance and support. Often just your presence is sufficient to help a person who needs your encouragement. The question you must answer regarding the use of your retirement years is how much of yourself you are willing to share. My own experience has proven to me the value and rewards of allocating as much of myself as possible.

I have seen many people find only emptiness in their retirement years because their lives lacked significance or the purpose to which they had given their lives wasn't sustainable. I have counseled many of them. Some of them had been talented achievers. I first ask them to make a list of the things they feel can bring them happiness. Then I ask them to make a list of what they consider to be their greatest talents, as well as their most rewarding accomplishments. We talk about the challenges they have faced as they have built their professional and family lives. I then invite them to use what they have learned from their successes to help and teach others.

I even invite them to share the wisdom they have gained from their failures. The lessons we learn from many of our failures are valuable and worth passing on. Without failure there would be no experience on which to build success. If you want to help another person, share your failures as well as your successes with him. It will encourage him to take the risks without which significant success is not possible and the important lessons are not learned. One of the finest ways to encourage another person is to show him how you overcame failures similar to his, and how you overcame fear and uncertainty to find success.

In your latter years, your greatest value—and your greatest reward—will be to share yourself with others. Your encouragement, your wisdom, and your generosity will be of immeasurable wealth to them. This is the completion of your calling.

To the Reader:

We enter the autumn of our lives with a treasury of deepened compassion, learned wisdom, and valuable experience to share with others. Decide how you will do that.

ACTION:

Decide Every Day What to Do with the Rest of Your Life

Our pasts are behind us, and we can do nothing to alter them. Our futures are before us, and we can shape them. One of the great deceptions that oppress us is the conviction that our futures have already been determined by our pasts. We are sentenced to a lifelong, relentless rut. If we have failed in most of our endeavors, we will continue to do so. If we have been highly successful, that trend will undoubtedly continue.

This is determinism that flies in the face of countless examples to the contrary. Why would a lawyer who repeatedly failed in his attempts to achieve political office continue to run? Because Abe Lincoln was to become one of our greatest American presidents. Fate didn't motivate him. Faith did.

THE MOST IMPORTANT QUESTION

The question for us all is: *What will I do with the rest of my life?* The answer is not a given fact for any of us. It is a choice we make. Every day.

There is a second deception that oppresses some of us about our futures. It is the view that when we reach a certain age, our usefulness has been exhausted. The euphemized term for it is *retirement*, something to which so many claim to aspire. Most enter this phase at a prescribed age at which Social Security benefits and company pensions are available. No longer wage earners, they consider themselves put out to pasture to spend the rest of their years being indulged and entertained. It's the reward at the end of the line. The expectation of their final years is to make no significant contribution to the lives of others or to the future of our world. These are the obligation-free years of lowered expectations.

What brought us to this state of affairs is a number of changes, too many to explore in full here. A prosperous economy, longer life spans, and a world of increasingly rapid change are among them. But there is something extremely insidious behind it all. It is the view that the wisdom of the years is not needed during the fads of today and by a world in constant value flux. It is the arrogance of the contemporary.

While we are not slaves to our pasts, neither are our past experiences and the education we've received throughout our journeys useless detritus to be discarded on the junk heaps of progress. The lessons we've learned, the skills we've acquired, and the networks of relationships we've built are assets of great value for our latter years.

ANSWERING THE QUESTION

All of which brings us to the question: what will you do with the rest of your life, particularly the years that follow your official working years? Are you aware of the value you can be to others by sharing your wisdom and experience with them? Each morning as you look at the face in the mirror, think of how you can add significance by using your wisdom, talents, and abilities in a way that contributes to the lives of others and makes this world a better place.

As you consider your future, think of it as an opportunity to make a positive difference. After all, you've spent your life equipping yourself. Thirteen years have passed since I reached sixty-five, and I consider those years the most rewarding of my life. Each morning begins with a five-mile walk. This is my time of meditation and prayer, a time when I ask God to enable me to help those I can benefit. I am constantly amazed by the people who come into my life, and I am thrilled to be able to share wisdom and encouragement. A lifetime of experience has equipped me to help them with their problems as well as their fear of failure. I can't imagine that there are many things more rewarding than helping others find and fulfill their purpose in life.

The average person begins their professional life with very little knowledge and virtually no experience. But they retire with an abundance of both. They know more than they have ever known and have more experience than they have ever had. They are equipped to do something significant. It would be unfortunate for such talented, knowledgeable persons to allow their talents and knowledge to atrophy through lack of use in the latter years. It would be a tragedy for them to allow their assets to lie dormant and un-invested. Yet, that is what happens all too often.

SOME GOOD EXAMPLES

Someone once asked the great cellist Pablo Casals why he still practiced his cello for hours each day. Casals was ninety at the time. He answered, "Because I have the distinct impression I'm getting better." Why does Jimmy Carter continue as a force for human rights around the world, long past his presidency? Why, because, the world cannot afford to lose his wisdom and experience or his passion for protecting the victims of brutality. The world needs the Casalses and the Carters, who shape a legacy for good to the end of their lives. The world also needs what you and I have to offer in our mature years.

What will *you* do for the rest of your life? The Old Testament prophet Joel spoke of old men who would dream dreams (see Joel 2:28). The New Testament church experienced a spiritual revolution that was to change the world and fulfill Joel's prophecy. Pentecost was not a youth movement. It included sons and daughters, young men and old men (see Acts 2:17). Yes, old men and women with a vision. Old men and women who would help change the world. Old men and women who are willing to make their contributions to God's emerging future.

William Booth, cofounder with his wife, Catherine, of this international organization to which I've committed most of my life, never considered retirement. His passion for the mission to which he had given his life burned hot to the end. While he gave over more and more of the details of the daily operation of the Salvation Army to others as he aged, he remained the sage leader, sharing his vision, his wisdom, and his passion for the mission. Here are the words he spoke in the last public gathering he attended, shortly before he died: "While women weep, as they do now, I'll fight; while little children go hungry, as they do now, I'll fight; while men go to prison, in and out, in and out, as they do now, I'll fight; while there is a drunkard left, while there is a poor lost soul upon the streets, while there remains one dark soul without the light of God, I'll fight—I'll fight to the very end."

To the Reader:

Every day we make our decisions about what we will do with the rest of our lives. What will you do to ensure that your calling guides you at the beginning of every day for the rest of your life?

ACTION:

Look Back in Gratitude, Forward in Expectation

It is good for us to look back on the journeys we've taken to appreciate where they have led us. For me personally, a day in April 1942 was decisive. On that day a team of horses pulled an old truck filled with our belongings through deep snow to an abandoned farmhouse in northern Minnesota that would be our home for the next twelve years. It now seems so long ago. So much has changed since then. Today there are few Westerners who can imagine what it would be like to live without telephone, electricity, running water, and indoor facilities. There are few who can imagine traveling on a wagon pulled by horses or cutting hay with a scythe or cooking on a woodstove or shoveling snow in order to open the barn door. But that was how it was on the farm where I grew from a boy to a man.

In that world, education was very limited and classes small. On the days I was actually able to attend school, I walked a long dirt road from home to school and back. Our teachers were honored and respected, and the lessons they taught were simple and straightforward. Everyone knew everyone else, and most were in some way related. In those days we traded our labor in place of money for the help we needed. The economy of life made most of us equal.

HONORING OUR PASTS

The past has a way of pulling us back to our beginnings as we remember how it was when we were young. I often think of those fences I built and how they defined the physical boundaries of my life, measured in acres and fields and woods. There were 150 acres under plow, 400 acres in woods and pasture, 50 acres in lowlands, 6 acres in gardens, and the balance in the road that led from the house to the front gate. My world consisted of 640 acres on the north end of Pine Mountain Lake. Though I certainly don't consider myself a prisoner to my past, I do want to honor it for how it helped to shape me. I remember it in gratitude.

I also want to remind myself of how far I've come and how much the world has changed. In my outer office I have four bookcases that contain many of the books I've read during my life. I've kept them as reminders of how differently I lived in the 1940s and 1950s and how much things have changed.

One that I cherish is our class yearbook, the book that our senior class published when we graduated from Backus High School. In this book the futures of our twelve graduating seniors were predicted by unanimous consent. Four of the twelve became ministers, three became teachers, three became social workers, one worked for a lumber company, and I became a management counselor. Six of us remain, and six have passed away. We've had a class reunion every five years since our twenty-fifth reunion, and all have been held in the fire hall in Backus.

I was twenty-one when I cast my first vote in the Grange Hall in Powers Township. Each township had its voting place, and there were thirty-eight eligible voters in our township. The old Grange Hall was used only on Election Day, which was always a social event. The coffeepot boiled all day on the woodstove, and the neighbors gathered and talked about their crops and the price of cattle and milk—and, of course, the opening of the hunting season.

Those were simple times, and most of the things that took place in the outside world were unknown to us. The county paper was our *New York Times*, and we read every word as though it were gospel. Our local telephone operator, who had the switchboard in her living room, was our town's reporter for the county paper. She got the news by listening to all the telephone conversations as she plugged them into the switchboard.

We were like one big family, everyone knowing exactly what was going on. No secrets could be kept. In many ways this was good, particularly in the wintertime, when most of us were snowed in. All of us were connected to one another. We knew we could speak with our neighbors and ask for help.

I was twenty-five when I left the farm, and twenty-five years were to pass before I would return. The land hadn't changed, but the buildings had burned in a fire several years earlier. I spent hours walking the fields and woods, remembering the time when this was my world. I hadn't returned sooner because my life on the farm had been so difficult and I was trying to forget the way I lived as a boy.

INDEBTED TO OUR PASTS

Now, as I've passed my seventy-eighth birthday, I appreciate those early years in a new way. The road to the years that followed was paved with the life-changing experiences of my time on the farm. I have learned that most tough experiences eventually bring a harvest of blessings. They condition us to take better advantage of the opportunities that do come our way.

As I reflect on the days of my youth, I realize that I was cultivating the soil of my future as I labored long days on the farm and hoped against hope, in the providence of God, to realize my life's purpose. There were days of deep discouragement, but I clung to the hope, kept to the task, and prepared myself for the doors I believed would open.

I would not trade the experiences of my early years, nor those of the intervening years, for anything. They have shaped, sustained, strengthened, and satisfied me. They have taught me valuable lessons about how to live my life. Such as:

- I am responsible for my own life and development.
- I have been given the talents I need to fulfill the calling God has given me.
- I am responsible for developing and deploying my talents to realize my calling.
- My habits and disciplines will establish my character.
- I aim to exceed the expectations of others.
- I choose to give more than I expect to receive.
- I will go the extra mile but not require others to do the same.
- A positive attitude is essential for success.
- I choose to be generous with my compassion and committed to my friendships.
- I honor my commitments.

GRATITUDE FOR A LIFE PARTNERSHIP

As I look back over the years, I realize that my life has been blessed beyond measure more by people than anything else—people who have taught, encouraged, and cared for me. There is one who has meant more to me than these pages could possibly describe. I speak of Peggy, my wonderful wife, who has been my partner for these past forty-two years. What she has meant to me is beyond words. We have been partners in love, in business, and in adventure. We've worked hard together in projects large and small, and we've traveled the world together as well. I look forward to what still lies ahead for us.

I don't know how many more years I have in this life. What I do know is that today I have more to be grateful for than I deserve. In the words of Dag Hammarskjöld, I say, "For all that has been, thanks! For all that shall be, yes!" Under God's providence, I eagerly await my future.

To the Reader:

Look back over your own life and in gratitude and recall the persons and the experiences that helped you the most. Then look to your future. You can't predict the future but your gratitude for the past can help you visualize what the future can become. Believe that the God who has cared for you and given you a wonderful life will continue to lead you into a future worthy of your highest expectations and hopes.

POSTSCRIPT
Continuing the Legacy

I have shared with you the prayer that has guided me over the years: "Dear Father, help me find a significant purpose for my life." This prayer has been a constant companion. It has guided me when I needed direction. It has encouraged me when I was unsure of the way. It has steadied me in times of uncertainty. Most of the time I was unaware of how it was being answered or the form the answer was taking. Over time, however, I could see the answer taking shape. I could see providence unfolding and I kept on believing that God would answer my prayer—and He did.

As I approached retirement I realized that the fulfillment of my purpose would be a lifelong quest, and I knew the past would build the foundation for the future to which God was still leading me. I began spending more time sharing my experiences and the lessons they had taught me with those who might benefit from them. My life took on a new sense of meaning. I began to use the lessons of my experience to help others meet the challenges they faced and overcome the difficulties and disappointments they encountered. The more I did this, the more I realized my purpose might have dimensions beyond those I had previously imagined. Perhaps it could be fulfilled by extending even further the commitments that had guided my working life.

I began to ask God how I could give more of myself to help others. Even though I had given forty years of my life to the Salvation Army, I sensed there was more I could do. The answer came in the form of a wonderful opportunity that would enable me to serve the Salvation Army and its mission even beyond my lifetime—in fact, far beyond it.

This is the answer that came to me: the fruits of my financial investment efforts over the years would be used to establish the Jack McDowell School for Leadership Development at the Salvation Army's Evangeline Booth College in Atlanta, Georgia. This is the college where Salvation Army officers who serve in the Southern Territory USA are trained and where they and other Army personnel have continuing opportunities for training and education. This college is the cornerstone of the Salvation Army's work in the southern United States. Tens of millions of people have benefited and will continue to benefit from the dedicated services of men and women who receive their education and training in this remarkable program.

My latter years will therefore be committed to helping the Salvation Army develop a leadership training program that will continue to nurture the kind of spiritual and community leaders who have made this organization such a powerful force for good in the world. This is the lasting legacy I wish to leave this Army for God and for good. This is the completion of God's answer to my prayer for a significant purpose.

ABOUT THE AUTHOR

J ack McDowell served as the Salvation Army's management counsel for thirty-eight years. It has been said that Jack has raised more money than any other person in the world for the Salvation Army. Jack was born in Hollywood, California, and grew up on a dairy farm in northern Minnesota. As a youth he was active in 4-H Club work and received its two highest national awards. He was president of the Minnesota 4-H organization. His first fund-raising experience came when he raised the money to pay the mortgage on the county 4-H building. As a result of that experience he developed a unique fund-raising concept that enabled him to raise hundreds of millions of dollars for churches, colleges, schools and the Salvation Army. In the forty years he practiced his chosen profession, every capital campaign he conducted exceeded its goal by an average of 169 percent.

Since his retirement in 1998 he has devoted his efforts to mentoring men and women of all ages, helping them achieve greater success in their business and personal lives. Jack continues to work closely with the Salvation Army. In 2005 he